Cherish

The Love of Our Mother in Heaven

Volume 2

Curated by

Ashli Carnicelli
Trina Caudle
McArthur Krishna

Cherish, Volume 2: The Love of Our Mother in Heaven

Copyright 2024 by Ashli Carnicelli, Trina Caudle, and McArthur Krishna, editors

All rights reserved. Printed in the United States of America. No part of this book may be used or reproduced in any manner without written permission except in the case of brief quotations embodied in critical articles or reviews.

D Street Press, Portland, Oregon, 97239

Cover by Kate Purcell and Jaida Hancock
Design by Andrew Heiss
Layout by Jaida Hancock

dstreetpress.com
ISBN: 978-1-7342287-3-1

Dedications

Ashli Carnicelli

This volume of Cherish, I dedicate to my beloved Savior Jesus Christ's Mother, Mary. I love you with all of my heart. I remain your faithful and humble daughter in deepest reverence and gratitude.

Trina Caudle

To the girls in my Activity Days group and Young Women camp levels and even my Scout troop — we are daughters of Heavenly PARENTS, a Father AND a Mother, and They love and cherish us all.

McArthur Krishna

I called my husband today to thank him for not making me choose between marriage or the passions I can offer the world. He deserves this dedication (and many, many others).

Contents

~

	The Gospel Topics Essay	ix
	The Jesus Trail	1
1.	The Nature of God	39
2.	Beloved Spirit Children	71
3.	Cherished & Distinctive Doctrine	113
4.	A Mother There	147
5.	Side By Side	183
6.	Divine Nature & Destiny	209
7.	Work Together	243
8.	Designers of the Divine Plan	273
9.	Influences from Beyond	317
10.	Connection	353
11.	Eternal Prototype	419
12.	Sacred Knowledge	451
13.	Highest Aspiration	493
	Our Mother's Love	531
	Contributors	565

The Gospel Topics Essay

The heart of The Church of Jesus Christ of Latter-day Saints is that all human souls are the literal spirit children of God — Heavenly Father and Heavenly Mother.

The testimony of the Savior Jesus Christ is central to this doctrine, as He is the way, the truth, and the life for all people to return to our Heavenly Parents after our earthly lives.

The doctrine of unified Heavenly Parents has been taught since the Latter-day Saints organized as a church in the early 1800s. There is no official statement from Joseph Smith teaching that God is a married male-female couple, but there are many teachings by other Church leaders referring to this concept.

Eliza R. Snow and W. W. Phelps, two prominent writers when the Latter-day Saints migrated to Utah, further spread this knowledge through their poetry, essays, and speeches.

Recent generations, however, have not been directly taught the doctrine of Heavenly Mother working in conjunction with the Father for the benefit of Their children. A myth in the culture of membership arose in the 1960s that, out of respect, people should not discuss the belief that Heavenly Mother exists, let alone teach it in public settings and elaborate upon what that could mean for relationships in marriage and generally between men and women. This "sacred silence" has been erroneously taught as doctrine for decades.

In 2010, a team of researchers at Brigham Young University embarked on a search in historical records to find as many quotes as they could from Latter-day Saint leaders about Mother in Heaven. They did not find an injunction from a prophet or apostle that people must not speak of Her. Instead, they found hundreds of references to "Heavenly Parents" and our Eternal Mother God by prophets, apostles, and other church leaders over the entire history of the Church.

Their report served as the base for a Gospel Topics essay — doctrinal statements approved by the First Presidency to summarize historical teachings of the Church that may have become confused over time. The Gospel Topics essay titled Mother in Heaven was released to the public on October 23, 2015.[1]

"New Essays Address Topics on Women, Priesthood, Mother in Heaven," Church Newsroom, October 23, 2015, newsroom.churchofjesuschrist.org/article/new-church-essays-women-priesthood-mother-in-heaven.

Cherish: the Joy of Our Mother in Heaven and *Cherish 2: The Love of Our Mother in Heaven* have been guided by this Gospel Topics essay. In those few paragraphs, we find many statements of belief and doctrine about the nature of God and the eternal destiny of all people.

Many individuals have shared their joy, love, and faith in our Mother in Heaven within these books, and we hope their testimonies will strengthen you as well.

I've a Mother There

Lauren Palmer-Merrill

INTRODUCTION

The Jesus Trail

"I walk this path as a **beloved daughter** of Heavenly Parents, **divinely known** and **deeply trusted**. As a child of the covenant, I am eligible to **receive promised blessings**. I have **chosen** to walk with the Lord."

President Emily Belle Freeman[2]

---

[2] Emily Belle Freeman, "Walking in Covenant Relationship with Christ," October 2023 general conference. Young Women general president, 2023-present.

Eternal

President Russell M. Nelson's call to "Hear Him!" has been a recurring theme in recent years, emphasizing that stillness enhances our connection with Jesus Christ. My heart longed to discover what following these teachings might manifest in my life. I've found that the quiet moments of the early morning are a beautiful time to practice being still, to spend some uninterrupted silent time with my Savior.

One such morning, I posed Him a question in my thoughts, "By what name would You like me to address You during our sacred time together on these early mornings?" I wanted to be respectful, worshipful, and honoring. After presenting Him with several possible ideas, and after a reasonably long pause in stillness, I felt His voice resonate through my entire being. He said to me, "My name is ETERNAL! But you can call me Jesus."

The feeling that accompanied the name Eternal was infused with such divine majesty, power, and glory, and the tenderness and love expressed when He said that I could call Him Jesus was just as profound. I felt His desire for our relationship to be deeply personal, and that there is nothing more important to Him than our relationship.

After I heard and felt Him tell me His name, and that I could call Him Jesus, I felt another voice resonate through me which was unmistakably feminine and ancient. She simply said, "Dear child, you are so loved!" I believe that the love expressed to me at that moment was from our Heavenly Mother.

Spending quiet, sacred time with the Lord, as counseled by church leaders, led me to Jesus more powerfully than I ever anticipated. And Jesus led me directly to the sacred Divine Feminine, who revealed Herself and Her love for me directly to my heart. It wasn't expected or specifically sought for, but it was gifted anyway. The impact of this experience is still expanding in my life.

Scott Turner

Her Son at the Center

I asked God in prayer to show me when my Mother in Heaven influenced me in my need. I desired to recognize Her influence to continue nurturing my relationship with Her. In response, pictures came to my mind of sacred moments.

One evening of deep discouragement, She offered me a small flower, illuminated by a shaft of street light, to remind me of my Heavenly Parents' love. She assured me that They knew me and were present with me.

Another evening, as dualism and perfectionism overtook my mother heart, both of my Heavenly Parents offered me hope. He reminded me of His promises. She invited me to let go of my limiting constructs and to see and love with new eyes. In the sealing room of the temple, She opened my eyes to Her many spheres of influence — Her kingdoms, thrones, powers, and principalities. She revealed that womanhood includes infinitely more than the roles I had assigned to myself. She invited me to seek my voice, my gifts and desires, the things that bring joy to my soul. She encouraged me to expand and soar!

One sleepless night full of fearful and despairing tears, She reminded me to keep Her Son at the center of my journey. With His healing and redemptive love, He would wipe away my tears.

God answered my prayer, nurturing my soul

Jenn Michaux

The Love of God

When I think about walking the covenant path and clinging to the rod of iron, it is something that I always want to do. I cling to my Savior, Jesus Christ. I cling to the covenants I have made with Him. Not only does this keep me in close proximity with He who I love and adore with all of my heart; I also know where the rod of iron leads.

In Lehi's vision, the Tree of Life is symbolic of the Love of God. This love streams from Jesus Christ and from my Heavenly Parents. That means this love comes from my Heavenly Mother too. While I believe we can taste of this love here in mortality, I can't imagine a more joyful and happy day when I make it back into Her presence and back into the fullest measure of Her love.

Ashli Carnicelli

Swell

Nichole Marie

Perfect Family

No matter how broken or absent our earthly family relationships may be
When we come to know the Gospel of Jesus Christ
We find ourselves within three perfect family relationships—
A Father, a Mother, and a Brother
Who love us beyond comprehension.

Angela Ricks

> "Dignity and demeanor in our discipleship begin with understanding who we are. Literally and specifically, we are sons and daughters of Heavenly Parents. We look to our Brother Jesus Christ as our perfect example and seek to emulate the divine attributes He demonstrated throughout His life."

Sister Rebecca L. Craven, counselor in Young Women general presidency, 2018-23[3]

---

[3] Rebecca L. Craven, "The Dignity and Demeanor of Discipleship," BYU devotional, Provo UT, October 19, 2021.

Ripples of Light

Through halls unknown I wander far
To find my home beyond memories veil
Dark is the hall and lost I feel
My eyes downcast my head bowed
A warm light ripples along the floor
Unsure though I am still hope swells
I run chasing its warmth
Still the light remains far from grasp
To be seen yet remain unknown
A voice from times long forgotten
Whispers now to raise my head
Forward now I see beyond narrow halls
Hope swells as I see that place
Where I hear my Parents call
Heavenly Father and Heavenly Mother as one
Farther still must I tread
Yet like my Brother from the stars
Purposely will I stride
With hope I pray not to stray

Michael G. Metro

A Heavenly Pattern

~

Heavenly Parents
Earthly parents

Made in the image of God
Male & Female

Numbered & Known
Never ever left alone

God gave us families
to love, bless, and protect

God gave us day & night
Opposition in all things

Sun
Moon

Stars
Black hole

Dreamy
Dreary

Agency to discern
Intelligence to learn

They prepared a way back home through the Begotten One
Christ, Their Son

Inseparably connected
Beloved children

Heavenly Parents
equal One

Living now
Living then
Living with Them again

Striving for Oneness
A Heavenly Pattern
Repeating

Michelle Gessell

His Mother is My Mother

~

I have a testimony from what I learned during my search for Heavenly Mother. I wanted to know who She is so I could try to be like Her. She would be my ultimate female example!

There is very little written about Her anywhere—I could only find some poetry. I was annoyed at God ... that women don't get a female example to learn and follow. After a while, I put it to the side because I knew there wasn't anything concrete. There's not a lot we know about Her. I figured someday I'll know, but for now I don't get to know who She is and how I should be like Her. I was mad about it.

One day, I was listening to the Follow Him podcast by Hank Smith and John Bytheway, with Jenet Erickson. They talked about feminine characteristics and male ones, and she said that many times in the Savior's teachings, He referred to Himself as having these womanly characteristics! "As a hen gathereth her chickens under her wings," or "you will be reborn in me." She said, "It doesn't matter to God who you are, man or woman. He cares that you are trying to be like Christ!"

Christ is our example of who to be like! He is perfect and He is the all-encompassing example of His Heavenly Father AND His Heavenly Mother ... who are MY Heavenly Father and Heavenly Mother! I do have an amazing example to follow, and it's Jesus Christ. He's the one I should be trying to be like, because HE is everything SHE is. If I try to be like Him, then I will be trying to be like Them. Like HER!

Now I find little bits of information about Her, and see pictures and read poems, and it all points me to Christ in an even deeper way. I feel closer to my Heavenly Mother than ever before because I see Her in all the things I see my Savior in. I love flowers and gardening and I know my Savior loves everything He made. Every plant and flower. And I realize: He probably learned that from His Mother. My Mother.

Kayla Pennington

"Each of you is a beloved spirit son or daughter of Heavenly Parents. You do have a divine nature and destiny. During your premortal life you learned to love truth. You made correct eternal choices. You knew that here in mortality, there would be afflictions and adversity, sorrow and suffering, tests and trials to help you grow and progress. You also knew that you could continue making correct choices, repent of incorrect choices, and through the Atonement of Jesus Christ inherit eternal life."

Elder Randall K. Bennett, Seventy[4]

---

[4] Randall K. Bennett, "Choose Eternal Life," October 2011 general conference.

Mattatuck

I went to five years of Young Women Camp in western Connecticut, on a tree-covered hill that sloped down to a crystal clear lake. The annual hike was a trail from the fishing dock, around the edge of the lake, up to the top of a ridge and across the hill, to end near the kayak and canoe launch.

We never talked about the hike as a metaphor for life but it certainly was one.

The trail started easily but quickly became bumpy with rocks and tree roots, waiting to trip you. One section of the trail was so close to the edge of the water that if you slipped in the mud, you were getting wet. Another section was so overgrown that we went straight into the bushes and hoped to steer clear of poison ivy. At about the halfway point, on the opposite side of the lake from the camp, we stopped in a sunny clearing to rest our feet and eat snacks, and shout "HELLO!" across the water to hear the echo.

All along the way, friends walked and laughed together. On the ridge climb, they grabbed hands to pull each other up onto the larger boulders. And through it all, we had a guide who knew which way to go and all the secrets of the trail until we returned back to camp.

I'm grateful for our Guide through life, that we can follow the Savior home to our Heavenly Parents.

Trina Caudle

Every Step of the Way

~

After an especially challenging season in my life, I took a weekend away to catch my breath and re-charge. I just wanted to be free from the heaviness, and more than anything have my son's pain lifted. I found a cozy chair outside my AirBnB, and lay there basking in the sun.

I began pleading in my mind with my Heavenly Parents to lift this heavy cloud hanging over me. Colors began to flood my vision—dark, heavy colors moving like a muddy river and trying to pull me in. It felt so real, so vivid. I began to cry. A deep, gut-wrenching sorrow enveloped my entire body, as if all the pain of my son and every child suffering was weighing on my soul. I begged to be free from it, for them to be free from it.

It felt like a long time, but then the dark colors were gone and I had the most vivid image of my Savior at the foot of a tree, being cradled and held by His Heavenly Mother. And I wept. "Of course You were there," I said out loud to Her. "You were there all along."

Every cell in my body felt this truth, that She had been there every step of the way with Her Son. I sobbed at this realization and thanked Her over and over.

And then I realized that this meant She was there for my son as well, and She always would be. For all of the times I felt I had failed or come short as his mother, She was holding us both. And of course, so were my Savior and my Heavenly Father. I will never forget this experience. As I write about it, I am in tears again.

Andrea Weaver

She's Worth The Wait

∼

Today I found Her.

It has felt like a thousand lifetimes.

Waiting. Wondering.

Silently seeking.

Pondering. Praying. Petitioning.

Heartbreaking and healing.

They say a Woman is always worth the wait.

At times I wondered if that was true.

If I could feel fulfilled without knowing

Until I realized no one else could bring Her to me.

Once I chose to seek Her, My Mother, all notions put aside,

I felt of Her power, Her love, Her kindness and warm embrace.

I felt of Her omnipotence, Her wisdom, Her calm.

She too was patiently, perfectly waiting

To relieve my perfect storm

That lead me to Her, battled and broken and bruised.

She was worth the struggle, the pain, the agonizing wait.

She is the missing piece that made my heart whole.

The assurance that She gives me, the confidence in my bones.

The life in my every breath.

This testimony burning like fire.

Your silence breaks like thunder

When I stop and listen with pure intent to hear.

The stillness removes all doubt and casts out all my fear.

You work in Harmony with the Father and Your precious Son.

We all belong together, and a Woman's identity is divine.

I know I belong to You and all my sisters too.

You are with me every step, providing me all I need; Your words, Your Wisdom with all my Father's too.

Women and Men, prophets, prophetess', apostles, disciples all as a compass pointing me to Your stars

Most importantly provided a Savior to save me, to bring me home again.

You truly are guiding, protecting, reassuring my wild soul.

By finding You, Mother, I've found me.

Now I patiently rest with a firmness to endure

Till the perfect day I see Your face and radiance so pure.

I'm not afraid to say it now:

She's worth the wait,

Every minute that it takes.

I'm growing closer to Her through Her Son.

Glorious, one day I'll walk into Her presence.

I know now deep within my heart:

We are both worth waiting for.

Whitney Rose

Four Cords

A cord is stronger with more than one rope

One for the Father

One for the Mother

One for the Son

One for the Spirit

Four chords in every Song

Four layers of tissue in the human frame

Four cords of strength

For binding and sealing

The entire human family

Indestructible bonds

Held fast

Four cords of Love.

When I think about my Heavenly Father and my Heavenly Mother working together for the salvation of the human family, side by side, I think about how much stronger a rope is with two cords rather than one. And then I think about how our Savior Jesus Christ and His Spirit are a part of this great work.

Ashli Carnicelli

Haitian Heavenly Mother

Lovely McArthur

Trial

A few years ago, I learned that my husband of 14 years had been having affairs with other women. I was completely devastated and felt abandoned and not good enough. I felt as if no one else knew what I was going through, even though my Savior Jesus Christ did.

Fortunately, I had followed a prompting a year prior to start building a personal relationship with my Heavenly Mother. I didn't know how important that relationship would become, but I cultivated it because I felt that I should!

The presence of Mother was so strong in those beginning months. I could feel Her embrace when I thought I might die from the pain I was feeling. She was there to hold me close when my faith was on the brink of being obliterated. I felt Her through the kindness of the sisters and brothers in my life who showed up, through songs that would play on the channels I listened to, and in the numbers '143' that I suddenly saw everywhere—which equal the letters in the words "I Love You."

Our Mother cares. She cares about what is going on in our lives. She cares about how we feel. She loves seeing us happy and She can comfort us when we are in the pits of despair.

Our Savior Jesus Christ will lead and point us to our Heavenly Parents on high, and direct us to the path that can lead us back to Them.

Lily Jeneal Landon

Some Days

Some days you just need a hug from your Heavenly Mother and Her wisdom in your hand, some grounding from your Savior, and some sturdy reassurance from your Heavenly Father.

When I just need a little more...

I see Heavenly Mother represented in a tree located in front of our local ward building. I've affectionately dubbed it my Mother Tree.

I see the Savior represented in the ground beneath my feet, and enjoy lying on the earth to feel His love and support.

And I see my Heavenly Father in the sturdiness of the building.

I love connection with all three. I touch each one, close my eyes, open my heart, pour out my heaviness, and stay connected until I receive a lightness inside instead. Simple yet powerful.

A beautiful reset or setup for a good day.

Emily Baker

Testimony of Heavenly Mother's Love

My experience with Heavenly Mother wasn't something I was searching or praying for. The topic of Heavenly Mother wasn't one that my heart yearned for at the time. But since this experience, it has been impossible for me to ignore. It has left me with so many questions, with confusion, but with a feeling of love I'd never felt before.

I was visiting my cousin in 2019—she grew up Baptist but had decided she no longer believed what she had been taught while growing up. She was trying to decide what God meant to her or if she believed in God at all. We talked about various religions and different ways to view God. In frustration, she said, "I don't get it. Why is God only male or masculine? Why does Christianity deny the existence of Divine Feminine?"

I instinctively began to explain, "Actually, we believe something different than other Christian faiths. We believe that we have a Heavenly Father and a Heavenly Mother. We believe that our Heavenly Mother loves us with a love that we can't truly comprehend. Just as an earthly mother, She's intently listening and She's in the details of our lives."

While I was saying this, my eyes began to water and a familiar yet completely new feeling filled my chest. It caught me by surprise! It was the same thing I felt many times as a missionary, but more! There was a pause and a feeling of love. She just looked at me and said, "Mormons are so weird ..." We laughed and the conversation went on.

Later that night I stayed awake trying to make sense of what I had felt. I thought, "I think the Spirit testified to me the truth of Heavenly Mother's love." As a missionary, I testified many times of Christ's love, of Heavenly Father's love, and an undeniable feeling of the Spirit would confirm what I was saying was true. Until this conversation with my cousin, I had never testified nor heard a testimony of Heavenly Mother's love. The opportunity had never presented itself and I didn't know it could be done.

As I had shared with my cousin what I knew about Heavenly Mother, I felt a love that I hadn't felt before. The only way I can describe it is: complete. It was a love I didn't know was available, or even existed. I didn't know I was missing it until I felt it. The Spirit spoke to my heart, "Yes, She's real! She truly exists and She truly loves you just as much as your Heavenly Father and Savior love you."

Since that day, my eyes and heart have opened to the truth that there's more love to be received! My Heavenly Father's love and my Savior's love have guided and healed me throughout my life, but I now recognize there is a necessary and complete love available that includes my Heavenly Mother.

Sonia Sosa-Rollins

Beautiful World and Plan
Sing to the tune of "Beautiful Savior"

～

Fair is the Mother, Fair is the Father, enrobed in the love of eternity

Them will I honor, praise and give glory, Spirit Parents of my divinity.

He said, we shall be one. She said, it shall be done. And the stars of heaven newly born began to sing:

Beautiful Savior, conceived through Godly love, born to redeem all humanity.

Beautiful world and plan, set forth by Gods above, Mother and Father, we long to see,

We will follow Christ's way into eternity, and with our families, we'll always be.

Kayla Gisseman

1
The Nature of God

"This understanding is rooted in scriptural and prophetic teachings about the nature of God, our relationship to Deity, and the godly potential of men and women."

~ Mother in Heaven essay, paragraph 1

She Is A Force

∽

She is a wonder
She is indescribable
for Her attributes have no limit
and cannot be contained by the finite
bounds of human language

She is a power
She is immutable
She is everlasting
She is the rush in (of) the ocean current
She is the strike of a lightning bolt
She is the brilliance of the sun
In Her is the very resonance at the center
of the universe
The boom of tectonic plates shifting and
colliding
She is the life force of the earth
Of human life, She gave Her breath
She is sovereignty.

Alexandra Williams

The Destiny of Godhood

"Sisters, the doctrine says you are not some twisted version of Heavenly Father. You are a perfect version of Heavenly Mother. Your destiny is not first counselor-hood. Your destiny is Godhood." Mike Goodman, BYU professor

The clarity of revelation described in Doctrine and Covenants 8:2—"Yea, behold, I will tell you in your mind and in your heart, by the Holy Ghost ..." has always been literal for me. And I had that clarity when I found this quote from Brother Goodman.

I am not and have never been some twisted version of Heavenly Father or a man. I am not destined for first-counselor-hood, a sidekick to my husband.

I am in the image of Heavenly Mother, who has equal power, authority, and love in partnership with Heavenly Father.

Trina Caudle

She Is God

She is God. We are humans.

Good thing we believe Heavenly Mother is a God, because otherwise, who does that mean I am in the next life? Some lesser being? A handy hand-maiden? A lady to run heavenly errands for all eternity?

I laugh as I write this ... so calm in my knowledge that I am made in Her image, the image of my God Mother.

McArthur Krishna

Heavenly Mother Watching Over Her Children

Emily Carruth Fuller

Central to our Religion

I realized that what was missing from my current spiritual understanding was an awareness of the connection between divine motherhood and the atonement of Christ! I have come to believe that the two are inseparable.

There are many scriptures in which Jesus's love and care is compared to that of a mother's: Luke 13:34, 1 Nephi 11:20-23, 3 Nephi 10:4-6. Therefore, if the atonement of Christ is central to our religion, a true understanding of Heavenly Mother is too.

Frazer Cluff

> "There is radiant warmth [in the] thought that ... [we have] a Mother who possesses the attributes of Godhood. ... Since we have a Father, who is our God, we must also have a Mother, who possesses the attributes of Godhood."

Elder John A. Widtsoe[5]

---

[5] "Everlasting Motherhood," *Millennial Star* 90, May 10, 1928: 298; and *A Rational Theology: As Taught by the Church of Jesus Christ of Latter-day Saints*, (Salt Lake City: Deseret Book, 1937), 69.

What They're All About

To me, the reality of the existence of Heavenly Mother is a beautiful and powerful doctrine. It is inspiring. Knowing She exists opens my eyes to more of what eternal life, eternal marriage, and eternal families are all about and why they are so important. I have a testimony that in this dispensation this doctrine was originally revealed to and taught by the Prophet Joseph Smith.

Tyler Mills

Love Colored Glasses

J. Kirk Richards

My 14th Article of Faith

~

I believe in the Eternal Mother,

Her equal partner Heavenly Father,

and in Their Son, Jesus Christ,

and in the Holy Ghost.

She is virtuous,

lovely,

of good report,

praiseworthy,

and I seek after Her.

I can become like Her.

She loves Her children,

and She wants us to return to Her.

Mother and Father sent Their Son to bring us home.

Malinda Wagstaff Metro

The Forgotten Divine Life Weaver

∽

Beyond human gaze dwells a Heavenly Mother, cloaked in the celestial tapestry of glory and eternity. Her essence, often veiled, bears the profound weight of cosmic wisdom and nurturing grace.

She emerges as a Creator not only of life but as a Weaver of existence's very fabric. Her unseen hands traverse the cosmic loom, crafting constellations that narrate tales of love and resilience. Within Her embrace, the universe finds its equilibrium, a harmonious dance, and purposeful existence.

Heavenly Mother, concealed in the shadows of history, transcends the confines of earthly narratives. She is not a mere footnote but the author of our souls' odyssey, penning stories of valor and persistence in the eternal chapters.

Her silence, often misconstrued as absence, testifies to Her profound wisdom, for in contemplative quietude, the deepest truths unfurl. Her voice, a gentle murmur in the cosmic zephyrs, guides us toward self-discovery, urging us to seek enlightenment and wisdom.

She embodies divine feminism, a beacon of both strength and compassion. In Her, we uncover the archetype of empowerment, not in defiance of the masculine but within the harmonious union of complementary forces.

Her presence serves as a reminder that true equality springs not from the suppression of disparities but from the celebration of diversity.

Guillermo Lemus

A Revelation's Birth

In the quiet moments when hearts inquire,
The world stirs with a celestial fire.
A Heavenly Mother, long veiled from view,
Emerges in whispers, saying "it's true"

In the dawn's soft glow, a revelation's birth,
The world awakens to a truth of sacred worth.
A Heavenly Mother, in shadows long concealed,
Her presence in our hearts, now fully revealed.

Her love, like the sun, a radiant embrace,
In every corner of creation, Her grace.
In the whispers of wind and the songs of the dove,
The world awakens to the Feminine above.

In this knowledge, a sacred unity we find,
A Mother's love, eternally kind.
To discover Her is like feeling the sun
To discover Her is to feel as one

Carly White

Ibeorgun

I served my mission, in part, among the Cuna people of Guna Yala, an island chain off the coast of Panama. Their indigenous culture has a strong oral tradition. Among their stories are accounts of the visit of Ibeorgun, a "great white god" who came down from the sky and put twelve men in charge. But on some of the islands, their story about the great white god is a little different, and one of the sweetest things I heard. They say there that Ibeorgun was not alone when he came down to visit the people from heaven: instead, he came down with his wife.

I've always thought that was beautiful.

Nathan Young

Aware of Every Tear

Jennifer Alvi

Who is She?

~

She is that She is
And whispers
(Cries out if She must)
You are that you are!

Yes,
I finally hear the message
Piercing the incessant hollers,
all telling me who I should be

The one truth She knows my heart needs
more than any other
The key to it all
The homing beacon
Calling us to ourselves

I am that I am
I am that I am
I am that I am

Just
like
Her.
And every soul
Every
Single
Soul

Each
Her child
Each
She birthed
Each gasped their first
Breath of life
And began to forget.

What is the divine feminine to me?

It is remembering

Grasping at a fading dream
Trying to wake and live
And not forget
Her blazing eyes
Reflected in my own

Chelsea Bowen Bretzke

> "We were created ... in the image of our Father and our Mother, the image of our God."

President Brigham Young[6]

---

[6] *Discourses of Brigham Young*, editor John A. Widtsoe, (Salt Lake City: Deseret Book, 1954), 51.

A Pastiche of "The Runaway Bunny"

~

The story of "The Runaway Bunny" by Margaret Wise Brown reminds me of our Heavenly Mother. Although several of Her children have forgotten Her or don't desire to include Her in their lives, She is always there for us.

Once there were children who had to leave their home for a while. "When you leave," said their Mother, "I will still care for you. For you will always be my children."

"What if when we leave," said the children, "we turn into orcas and swim far from You?"

"If you turn into orcas," said their Mother, "I will be a lady who walks on the sea, and I will come to you."

"If you are a lady who walks on the sea," said the children, "what if we turn into screech owls, flying high into nests in tall trees?"

"If you turn into screech owls, flying high into nests in tall trees," said their Mother, "I will transform into a blind snake and I will slither up to your nests and help you."

"If you transform into a blind snake," said the children, "what if we turn into yellow carnations in a secluded garden?"

"If you turn into yellow carnations in a secluded garden," said their Mother, "I will transform into a bee. And I will fly to you."

"If you transform into a bee and fly to us," said the children, "what if we turn into tree trunk spiders and scurry elsewhere?"

"If you turn into tree trunk spiders and scurry elsewhere," said their Mother, "I will be the tree that you make your home in."

"If you are a tree," said the children, "what if we turn into sailboats, and float far from you?"

"If you turn into sailboats and float far from me," said their Mother, "my breath will be the wind and I will guide you to where you need to go."

"If your breath is the wind that guides us," said the children, "what if we become heavy sea turtles and plod away from you?"

"If you become heavy sea turtles and plod away from me," said their Mother, "I will be the moon and I will beam my light down to you."

"If you are the moon and beam your light down to us," said the children, "what if we turn into rabbits and run inside a burrow?"

"If you turn into rabbits and run inside a burrow," said the Mother, "I will transform into a doe and create a nest and snuggle you."

"Well then," said the children. "It sounds like You will always be near us, no matter what. We will always be Your children.

And so they were.

"Have some cake before you leave," said the Mother.

Darci Garcia

They Are Always Near Me

Kayla Becknuss

Very Little

~

I think this doctrine of Heavenly Mother is necessary to complete our relationship to God. We may not know much about God, the Mother, but the truth is we know very little about God, the Father also.

Benjamin Bardsley

What Kelsie Learned From Her Father

she told me she would go to him

with all her questions:

vast, far-reaching, eternally

important questions.

to each one, he gave the same response:
"well, what is the nature of God?"

now, I asked questions of my Father:

vast, far-reaching, eternally

important questions

to each one, He gives the same response:
"well, what is the nature of God?"

then He steps aside, and I see Her, too.

Danielle Kemp Nelson

Sometimes

sometimes

i don't like the lessons i'm taught

sometimes

all i hear is "he"

what about her?

i just don't

understand

why would we take away her voice?

she's not too fragile

she's strong

she's a creator

Elise, age 14

Power We Cannot See

This 2014 abstract Heavenly Mother painting plays on the microscopic images of mitochondria, the powerhouse of the cell. We don't know much about Her, but we know She has power that we cannot see.

Julia B. Blake

Mother to the Stars

With silver arms and midnight hands, She pulled in outstretched reach

The lapping waves and hushed surf to bare the hidden beach.

Deep from the sand, She formed a star and raised it to Her breast

And nursed it dear and tenderly, just as She had the rest.

She helped it grow under Her touch, with wisdom She did guide.

Each stage of growth, each mature phase, filled Her with love inside.

The time had come—it always has—for Her to say goodbye.

Reluctantly, She held Her babe, then perched it in the sky.

Kim Siever

Who Heavenly Mother is to Me

A still, quiet voice

Someone who gathers Her spirit children in like a mother hen

She offers love unconditionally

A feeling of love, caring, and warmth

Speaks to us spiritually

Knows our needs

Protects us throughout our life

If we seek Her, She provides a quiet place through life's trials from beginning to end

Trusts us with our choices

Understands Heavenly Father's eternal plan for us and is His partner in the plan

Surrounds all Her spirit children with Her love

Has Goddess beauty that shines from within

Possesses Godly attributes of mercy, humility, forgiveness

A person who feels happiness and joy for Her spirit children

With Heavenly Father, welcomes Her children to the Celestial Kingdom, offering happiness and joy for those making the journey there

Janice McArthur

Finding God

In finding Heavenly Mother, I have felt connected to God in a whole new way. I also have found more God in me! I am more patient, I am more kind, I have more love because She is in my life. She is good! Maybe I am too.

Carlie Webb

2

Beloved Spirit Children

"The Church of Jesus Christ of Latter-day Saints teaches that all human beings, male and female, are beloved spirit children of heavenly parents, a Heavenly Father and a Heavenly Mother."

~ Mother in Heaven essay, paragraph 1

Be Like Them

March 1, 2024 was the opening night for the art show I curated: Be Like Them, pulled from the President Oaks quote, "Our highest aspiration is to be like them." That's what all of this messy, chaotic, challenging, invigorating, and luscious life experience is for—to BE LIKE THEM.

To look around the gallery with over fifty pieces of art depicting our Heavenly Parents, and see the line to enter stretch down the street and around the corner, with over a 30-minute wait to just get in the door, it is CLEAR: people are hungry to know more of their Parents, and to celebrate that we are all Their beloved children.

One of my favorite pieces is a birdseye view of a boisterous dinner scene by Emily Fox King. It richly illustrates that ALL are welcome at our Heavenly Parents' table, and THAT is the point of the show. Being LIKE THEM, being Their beloved children, means we need to welcome ALL to our table, now.

McArthur Krishna

Part of the Holy Family

~

There is something so tender
About being a part of this family—
Heavenly Father
Heavenly Mother
Jesus Christ
The Holy Spirit

I'm Their daughter
I belong
We are a family
My seat can never be taken
It hasn't been earned

They love me so much,
And I love Them
I can feel it all around
Buoying me through my days
I matter to Them
No earthly opinion matters—
It is Their counsel I seek only
I seek to love Their laws
And live under Their roof again someday
I want to be near Them
Always.

Ashli Carnicelli

She Came to Me

She came to me when i asked

God how the stars and rainbows

and flowers of all colours were

breathed into perfect existence.

She came to me when i asked

how i could best serve Her children

who needed a soft gentle touch

when the world was hard, unyielding, and closed off.

She came to me when i asked

for a light feather touch on my head

when my world was 'too much'

to allow me to sleep in heavenly peace.

She came to me when i asked.

Kate Rees Evans

Comforted

The Mother wraps me in a blanket of stars,

Her hand pressing the glow of heaven to my shoulder.

I close my eyes and breathe in slowly.

My lungs fill with the aromas

Of smoke from a fire, baking bread,
And something else I can't quite place.

Her voice warms me from the inside like mulled cider.

Her whispered words like water falling over rocks.

"I know, my child, I know," She says.

"Everything will be alright."

Brittany Cromar

Wrapped in the Cosmos

I love the part of Jeremiah 1:5 that says, "before I formed thee in the belly I knew thee." I picture that, and am in awe imagining the time we spent being raised in Heaven. With all the power around Her, Heavenly Mother could have wrapped us in the very cosmos themselves, as She pulled us onto Her lap, cared for us and nurtured us.

Ashley Mansfield Hoth

Elijah and His Mother

1 Kings 19

Sacrificial dreams and a crooked neck—
Elijah slept under the desert juniper.
His request to die
had been denied.
This prophet thing was hard
and he was no better than his fathers.

And then She came
and touched him with cool fingers.
Watery angel soothing his sleep,
softening his aches
and washing away his nightmares,
tucking him into a bluish quilt,
and singing a quiet song.

He stirred and She whispered
Arise and eat
I have home water,
peanut butter and jelly,
and apples from the garden.
You'll feel better if you eat something.
He did, and She was right.

And so
pushed on by Her wave goodbye,
he went in strength to meet his Father,
a song stuck in his head
and a sandwich in his bag,
from the busy Gift-giver of the desert.

Up on the mountain,
his Father wasn't in the wind
or the earthquake or the fire,
but in the still small voice.

And Elijah's Mother
was in the long nap,
and the common sense,
and the peanut butter and jelly sandwich,
waiting under the Juniper.

Sarah Emmett

A Vicarious Hug

While doing inner child work

Connecting with and loving my little girl self

I imagined her sitting on my lap

I wrapped my arms around her, held her,

loved her and stroked her hair

I told her I understood how she felt,

that I knew her hopes and fears

The ones she wasn't brave enough to share

The ones she thought no one would understand

I told her how I was here for her now

How I had grown up

but I still remembered how she felt

And I'm always going to be here for her now

As I re-parented myself and created

A safe and loving relationship with myself

I felt Heavenly Mother behind me

wrapping Her big warm arms around me

with long hair around us both like a blanket

I knew in that moment that my Heavenly Mother was also there for me in all the ways

I was trying to love my inner self

She knows me and loves me

Just how I need, whenever I need

And always reminds me I am good

Just as I am

Years later, after sharing a healing moment with

One of my adult daughters — holding her from behind,

crying, rocking, slowly breathing together,

supporting her, loving her—

I remembered my experience of Heavenly Mother holding me

Tears crossed my cheeks as I suddenly

wanted my own earthly mother to hold me in the same way

I thought it could be strange, a request I hadn't made before

But I know my mother—

she's love in human form

She's basically a big warm hug herself

So at 46, I invited my mom to hold me

to hug me from behind

To support me and help me physically feel her love

And vicariously I felt my Heavenly Mother's hug

Jill Freestone

> "Knowing we lived before this life as beloved sons and daughters of Heavenly Parents enables us to take our personal identity from our divine origin."

Elder Robert D. Hales[7]

---

[7] Robert D. Hales, "The Plan of Salvation: A Sacred Treasure of Knowledge to Guide Us," Ensign, October 2015.

The Mother Seed

I

Once a little girl,
I was content
to know She
existed.
The idea of Her
was like a
beautiful little
seed.

As a teenager
and young mother,
I kept that seed in my
back pocket, happy
to know She was
out there ... somewhere.

But in recent years,
I have felt drawn to that seed
placed in my hand and heart
so long ago.
What kind of seed is it? I wondered.
What roots and branches could it grow?
What fruit will it bring into my life?

And so I planted it. And it grew.
It has rooted me and it has stretched me.
It has taught me the art of trimming and pruning.
And it has brought forth the most marvelous fruit.

II

Heavenly Mother
is like a zucchini seed.
Once you plant Her, She
will spread and claim space
with Her fantastic growth.
And every time you look,
there will be new
fruits waiting for you.

You will have to start
finding neighbors to
share your fruit with.
And when there aren't
enough takers,
you will take your fruit
into your kitchen and
grate it and mix it and

bake it into loaves
just to share your
bounteous harvest.

And your friends
and neighbors
will eat of it and
will know it is
delicious to the taste
and very desirable.

III

Heavenly Mother
is like a pack of
wildflower seeds
strewn across
an open field.

Give Her a little time,
some sun and rain,
and you won't believe
what will blossom
right before your eyes.

As you gather the flowers,
your house and your heart
will be filled to the brim
with the beauty and scent
of a Mother's love.

Rebecca Young

Kitchen Table

I hope Heaven has a kitchen table

Where my feet can dangle from the too-tall chair

While I eat warm chocolate chip cookies

And tell my Mother about my day

Alyssa Wilkinson

Daughters

Through my daughters—these noble and great ones—I am coming to know our Mother.

Each came to this life to bless me and point me back to Her.

These souls, valiant in the cause of truth, have come to teach me in beautiful ways.

My sisters before this life, for whom the veil is thin, gently link arms with each other and me, walking back into Their Holy Presence on the covenant path paved by our Savior.

Elaine Summers Horejs

In Her Image: Afghanistan

~

Anita Eralie Schley

Divine Eternal Duet

When I said goodbye to my Spirit Mother,
Did we cry together and make the ocean?
Did She promise She'd be there for me?
Did I know then that I'd ever question?

I emerged screaming,
My second mother's body contracting
violently.
It knew the inevitable,
And I fought it.

This Earth mother, she left me a scar
To remember her always.
It's where I was first fed
And last attached.

I left her scars, too.
Streams of pink on her stomach,
A walk through her own Gethsemane,
A body stretched and broken.

Did my Heavenly Mother leave me a scar
To remember the times I walked by Her side,
When She told me about Earth,
And growing up and going down?

Did I leave Her body
Scarred and stretched,
Enough to make
Even a Goddess reminisce?

And now my children,
My blood in another's body,
Fresh from heaven
They bring Her scent with them.

She whispers, "see them as I do."
They were Hers first, and forever.
Partners now in a divine duet,
We walk together again.

When I am born into the next life
And see Her again,
Will I come screaming, as with Earth?
Or will I sing when I die?

Ashley Masters Wilkes

You Are Loved

You are beautiful.

Even with your round belly stretched out and stretch marked with squishy skin from having so many babies.

You are beautiful.

Even with the extra 9 pounds on the scale,
Or your wrinkles
Or the times when you get a 71 on an exam
Or the times when you lose your patience with your children

You are beautiful

You are loved

Even on your worst days
Even when you feel you aren't your best,
Especially on your worst days,
Especially when you feel you aren't your best,

You are loved;

Because
you are loved
by a perfect
Mother.

Ashli Carnicelli

This Truth I Know

A loving King lives on high;

My Father,

This truth I know.

A loving Savior came to save my soul;

My Brother,

This truth I know.

But what of my Queen Mother? How can I know?

I see Her in the earth around me; the water, the gentle breeze, the moon in the sky.

I feel Her warmth in the women around me who uplift and support.

I smell Her in the newly fallen rain and in the flora surrounding me.

I hear Her in my heartbeat and in the very blood pumping through my veins, as I go about Her work.

I taste the bitterness of Her longing to connect with us while we are away from Her, and the sharpness of those wanting to find Her sweet fruits.

A loving Queen lives on high;

My Mother,

This truth I know.

Lily Jeneal Landon

Under Her Wings

~

Caitlin Hammond

Night Terrors

My children
Thrash
Crying out
Mumbled explanations
Eyes closed
Still dreaming
I—the here and now mother
Fill in
Hushing
Holding hands
Rubbing legs
Patting tummy full of gas
Until they surrender to sleep
and I lay awake
missing Her too

Chelsea Bowen Bretzke

> "We are beloved daughters of Heavenly Parents. We are disciples of Jesus Christ. We stand as a witness of God. Together we will be like a symphony—a rich and enveloping melody that reminds us of our divine identity and purpose as covenant women. ... Because of our divine and supernal Savior, Jesus Christ, we are glorious."

President Bonnie H. Cordon[8]

---

[8] Bonnie H. Cordon, "The Beautiful Reality of What it Means to be a Daughter of God," BYU Women's Conference, April 2021.

Mother's Sorrow

My hands cradle her tiny head,
dark hair surprising still
and the cracks in my heart
spreading deeper—

"I can't leave her," I weep,
my mother peering
over my shaking shoulders.

My days off will reach an end
in a few fleeting weeks

then she will spend so much of her life
in someone else's arms
in someone else's home.

I gaze out the window and wonder
if Mother felt the same
knowing the necessary send-off,
our temporary separation,
loomed ahead.

In the end
it would be what I needed,
but ...
did it hurt Her too?

Did tears fall freely
as She counted down
the days, the hours

til I would hold no memory of Her?

If my affection and protection
for this little soul
is anything like Her love for me,
then perhaps
I know the answer.

Lauren Madsen

In Her Image – Through A Kaleidoscope

18x24 inches, acrylic on panel

I'm told I was created in Your image
But I'm not sure what that looks like
Are You me?
but fuller?
I'm told I was created in Your image
But I'm not sure what that looks like
Are You me?
but fuller?
Rounder?
Darker?
I don't yet know
Or rather
I don't yet remember
So for now
I look at You
through a kaleidoscope
A mix of all the shapes and colors I see
in the daughters around me.

Carly White

One by One

Like many, I look forward to the time when we receive more revelation about our Heavenly Mother. In this current quiet space, however, we have the opportunity to come to know Her uniquely and personally, as She mothers us individually, one by one.

Angela Ricks

Saying Goodbye For Now

DeAnna Christensen

You Are

You are

You are loved

You are beloved

You are everything I imagined

You are everything I hoped for

You are who I created you to be

You are a blessing to humanity

You are a gift to the world

You are a part of me

You are mine

You are you

You are

Mari Christina Tomkinson Heward

Litter Box After A Long Day

It's been a long day. Long day of taking care of little ones. Long day after learning of the most recent injustices and degradations poured out upon the women of this planet. Long day of feeling less-than in all facets of my life. I am frustrated at my feeling of helplessness to change anything for the better. I complain about all of this to God while I clean out the litter box. My interior monologue is a muddle of angry phrases as I savagely scoop and shake the litter.

Then, slicing through the muddle in my head, I hear Them say, "You are not a second-class citizen in the kingdom of God." Their voices are so clear and unified and powerful. I know that is not coming from myself—it is my Heavenly Parents.

I still have long days. I still feel angry and helpless and less-than. But I remember that night of cleaning out the litter box and know that to Them, I am not less than anyone.

Darci Garcia

Bright Face

When I look upon Her face, I see divinity.

When I am alone with Her, I feel affinity.

Silver beams caress my face, and blue rays soothe me. As She passes sleeping earth, She nods approvingly,

Gently guiding owl and wolf and 'possum, hare to see.

Strength and pow'r alone She wields to pull and bear the sea.

Vacillate 'tween life and blood in lunar harmony.

As a Mother to the stars, yet watching over me.

Kim Siever

3

Cherished and Distinctive Doctrine

"The doctrine of a Heavenly Mother is a cherished and distinctive belief among Latter-day Saints."

~ Mother in Heaven essay, paragraph 1

Treasures of Knowledge

From a young age, my experiences in church led me to believe that being female was second to being male. After years of struggle, I concluded that maybe heaven wasn't for me. During this period of despair, I listened to President Nelson encourage us to ask the Lord our deepest questions. He asked, "What wisdom do you lack? What do you feel an urgent need to know?" My deepest questions were quite simple. Am I equal? Will I be equal in heaven?

So I asked, and when the answers came, I was overcome. A mystery was unfolding as the Lord revealed Mother in Heaven. What I learned was illuminating and empowering. As I sought to know more about Her nature, I looked to my own nature as a mother. From this exercise, I learned precious truths about Heavenly Mother, all of which we claim as doctrine.

First, She loves ALL Her children with a perfect love. Second, She watches over Her children and is involved in our lives. Third, our eternal destiny is Her work and Her glory. Fourth, Heavenly Mother is "side by side with the divine Father." They enjoy equal power and glory in heaven.

Through this process, I have learned that we are not meant to live in the dark. We have the power to unlock treasures of knowledge that Heaven is eager to pour down. I will always be grateful for President Nelson's prophetic invitation to ask in faith. His loving encouragement gave me the nudge I needed to seek further light, and the Lord's answers relieved a lifetime of doubts. I no longer fear heaven; I want nothing but heaven.

Brittany Manjarrez

Real Fact

I am a member of the Church of Jesus Christ of Latter-day Saints. I have been a member for 52 years. I chose to join the Church when I heard the story of Joseph Smith Jr. from his history in the Pearl of Great Price. When I heard of the vision of God the Father and Jesus Christ in the grove, and the visit of Moroni to Joseph Smith in his bedroom, I knew immediately that story was true. It was a definite sense of knowing.

Much later, I learned of the doctrine of Heavenly Mother. When I heard this, I knew it was a real fact just as strongly as I know that Joseph Smith is a prophet, and that we have a Heavenly Father, and that Jesus Christ is the only begotten Son of God.

Don Mitchell

Cherish Is a Verb

~

It has become a running joke among my children that I collect art of Heavenly Mother and Rainbow Jesus. It has spilled out of our office and spread into our living room, library, and family room. I'm not fortunate to purchase original pieces, but I have prints by Rose Datoc Dall, J. Kirk Richards, Amber Eldredge, Charlotte Condie, and more.

What do you do when you cherish something? You don't put it in a storage room or avoid the subject. You give it a place of honor in your home and life. When I was a young adult, Church leaders encouraged us to have a picture of a temple in every room of our homes. I don't see this as any different.

So when you enter my home, there's no missing it that I cherish the doctrine that we have a Mother in Heaven, the doctrine that men and women are meant to be equal partners in the eternities, and the doctrine that Jesus loves everyone.

Trina Caudle

The Veil Has Burst – Seek and Ye Shall Find

~

Megan Zabriskie Watson

Know and Respect

I know that I have a Heavenly Mother. I know that She lives and loves me. I am grateful for this knowledge because it helps me see my daughters, my wife and my sisters as gods created in my Mother's image. I respect my sisters and I want to treat them as I would treat a goddess.

Julio Ospina

General Conference

Every general conference, I like to take a question with me so I can get revelation. Lately, almost every question I take is about Heavenly Mother because She is very intriguing to me. I want to learn more about Her.

During the April 2022 general conference, I really wanted to hear something about Heavenly Mother. While I was thinking about this, Elder Renlund got up and began to talk about Heavenly Mother! I was so excited! As far as I know, he is the first person to talk about Heavenly Mother in general conference. It made me so happy! I noticed that he said he wants to learn more about Heavenly Mother, too, so we have that in common.

I'm so grateful Elder Renlund talked about Heavenly Mother in general conference.

Lecia Crider

> "Each of us is on a quest in this life to purify ourselves of mists and veils so that we may see truly and clearly into each other's hearts and there perceive that each one is a sister or a brother, equally a beloved child of our loving Heavenly Parents."

Sister Chieko N. Okazaki, counselor in Relief Society general presidency, 1990-97[9]

---

[9] Chieko N. Okazaki, *Sanctuary*, (Salt Lake City: Deseret Book, 1997), 57.

Patience

Most of the time spent

writing a poem

is silence.

Thought condensation

giving to life—

In(visible) action.

Most of the time spent

creating an earthly body

is waiting.

Gestating

for nine months

(not so?) patiently ...

Creation is not just

alive in the moment

of tangible arrival.

A cry, a laugh,
A lighting strike
of brilliance.
Creation exists
in still small moments
of waiting (patiently?)
How much of Her eternity
is spent in quiet waiting?
She must be patient.
Emerging as we condense
small droplets of ink
in Her long-awaited honor.

Erika Larsen

Finding Her Means I Too Have a Place

~

Jenna Conlin

Child, I am Here

When I prayed to know if God was real, my question used the words of a song: "Heavenly Father, Are you really there?" A Child's Prayer is a beloved children's hymn by Janice Kapp Perry sung with two parts, a child asking and a parent or teacher confidently answering, "Pray, He is there, Speak, He is listening." The two verses blend seamlessly, so that the question doesn't need to linger.

But on this night, I was no longer a child, not yet an adult, and my teenage heart held onto this question. It wasn't enough for others to tell me, "He is there ... He is listening;" I needed to know for myself. Kneeling by my bed, with the tradewind breeze whistling, I asked "... Are you really there?"

Before I could even finish the stanza, a different Primary song came into my mind. "Child, I am here, can you feel that Heaven is near?" That night, God was with me, and I felt Heaven's proximity.

This call and response with God continues. In quiet moments, I ask—and again I hear, "Child, I am here."

It was not until recently that I asked again, and this time, I realized who was speaking in the second song. The words are from Mother, Tell Me the Story, another song by Sister Perry with a similar format: a child asking and a parent responding. But it is not just a parent responding, it is explicitly a mother. My Heavenly Mother's love had been there when I needed Her, before I had been ready to know Her.

Josie Tueller

Grateful

How grateful I am that my church holds this as a cherished doctrine, clearly stating that we have a Heavenly Mother! As I have studied what the prophets and apostles have said about Her, I have gained a greater understanding of who I am and who I will become. Understanding my relationship to my Heavenly Mother has changed how I view myself.

Jill Freestone

In Her Image: China

Anita Eralie Schley

Care for the Doctrine

The tipping point for me came during a history course at BYU. It was one of the classes with over 150 students. I noticed the professor took the time at the start of class to carefully re-emphasize her faith, her professionalism, and her support of the Church general authorities. Why was she so suddenly cautious? The topic that day was feminism, both historically and in the present.

I had always seen feminism as a non-issue. Of course women should be treated equally and fairly! If someone had asked me if I was a feminist, I wouldn't have hesitated to say Yes. Who wouldn't be? So when a male peer bristled against the concept that women weren't treated the same way as men, I shrugged.

The professor responded carefully, explaining that inequality was still present in social and systemic settings, not just legal ones. But the student pushed back again. So the professor turned to the women in the room and asked: "Show of hands, how many of you carry pepper spray, or a taser, or put your car keys between your fingers when you walk to your car?"

Every single woman in the room put her hand up.

I was floored. I had never even thought about the necessity of any of that. Seeing that none of the men put their hands up in response to the same question, none of them had either. But it didn't stop there. The professor asked, "In this vein, what are other things women in this room do to keep yourself safe?" The responses came out like a tidal wave: Calling someone when they have to walk alone. Begging the city for more street lights south of campus. Never smiling at strangers. Taking self-defense lessons. The list went on and on, and I was stunned by how much thought they had to put into something as basic as existing in public in Provo, of all places.

This experience, along with the dozens of similar ones that came in its wake, led me to care deeply about the doctrine of a Heavenly Mother. It gives me hope that the heavens do not suffer from the same prejudices and blind spots that the world around me does. It gives me joy when my sisters and my wife can find purpose and value in the truth of the Divine Feminine—and I realize now that not everyone has always been able to see themselves reflected in the heavens.

Nathan Young

Cherish and Charity

The words cherish and charity have the same word root. This connection has been instructive to me as I have considered what it looks like for me to cherish my Heavenly Mother.

Word Root: ka: to like, desire

Cherish: to hold dear, to care for, nurture

Charity: the pure love of God that will endure and never fail (Moroni 7)

Cherishing my Heavenly Mother means I hold Her dear by actively seeking Her and nurturing an interactive relationship with Her. I feel Her love for me as I recognize Her influence in my life.

This outpouring of pure love nurtures an enduring relationship between us. Cherishing Her ignites my desire to speak of Her openly and confidently with respect and reverence, fostering growth in myself and others while gathering Her children into Her care.

Jenn Michaux

The Divine Feminine: Her Warmth

Kiley Yates

> "Establish in the mind of a young person the powerful idea that he or she is a child of God and you have given self-respect and motivation to move against the problems of life."

Elder Dallin H. Oaks[10]

---

[10] Dallin H. Oaks, "Powerful Ideas," October 1995 general conference.

Reflections on Grief

One of the most powerful moments that brought Heavenly Mother into my life happened just one month after losing my best friend, Alisa, in a car accident. As I sat on my couch one day, weighed down with crushing grief, I heard a voice speak softly to my heart: "She's with the Mother now."

Accompanying that thought was the deepest peace I've ever felt. For that one brief moment, the heavy grief lifted from my heart and I felt an intimacy with my Mother and a sweet nearness to my friend. I felt an increased connection to my Mother in Heaven knowing that my dear friend is with Her. I believe that they are both closer to me than I can know as I navigate my life without Alisa and strive to balance the grief of my loss with deep gratitude for twenty beautiful years of friendship.

Rebecca Young

My Feelings About "A Girl's Guide to Heavenly Mother"

~

It all started with my mom asking me and my sisters to go to this lady's house in our ward because she was going to have an author, McArthur, of a book called A Girl's Guide to Heavenly Mother speak to us. Honestly, I didn't really want to go, but I kept my mouth shut because I kind of had a feeling that I should go, so I just went along with it.

When we got there it started out a little boring, but after a few minutes, it started getting a lot more interesting and spiritual. When McArthur talked about how she came up with the idea, and how she and the book's editors found each other and got together to write it, I got a warm feeling inside, and I felt like a lot of my prayers were answered.

When it was over, I asked my mom if we could buy the book and she said, "yes." When we got home, I went straight to my room and started reading the book. I learned a lot of things and realized that Heavenly Mother is a big part of my life and is one hundred percent equal to Heavenly Father.

From then on, I've paid a lot more attention to Heavenly Mother and have felt closer to Her. That night, I even prepared and taught a lesson for our family about Heavenly Mother. I was so grateful that I went to that meeting and want to learn more about Heavenly Mother!

Eloise Bell

O My Mother

Heavenly Mother,
Are you really there?
Am I in Your image?
My potential, your divinity?

I AM a child of a Goddess!
And She has sent me here.
Co-creator of the Plan,
She knows my path on earth.

How great Thou art!
All powerful and knowing.
To think one day
I'll become like Her!

In the heav'ns are parents single?
No! My role models for
Equal partners
In purpose and parenting.

Dearest children, Mother is near you
Watching o'er you day and night;
Noticing, understanding,
Knowing deeply your soul.

Nearer, my Goddess, to thee;
I long to be embraced by You.
When I'm weary of this world
I want my Mom.

Where can I turn for peace?
When I feel the pain
Of a mortal mother misstepping —
She is a Perfect mother.

Be still my soul!
To know She's on my side!
Proud of me,
Cherished infinitely.

I know my Mother lives
And loves me too.
I'll aspire and strive
To come Home to You.

Amelia Dunn

Heavenly Embrace

For awhile, I have wanted to try painting my own version of who I think Heavenly Mother is.

I imagine Her skin and hair to be all the colors of light which, when combined, becomes white but shimmers with color and changes as She moves.

I think She would look young and strong, yet ageless, and, in Her eyes I could see a depth of love and wisdom that transcends age.

Most importantly, I wanted to portray Her as the embodiment of infinite love and compassion.

I often envision myself being held in Her embrace, and here, She is holding the child version of me, because I believe that I am still a child in Her eyes.

Rachel Jensen

Meaningful

Why would I not want to know and learn about my Mother? Myself, as I am writing this, I am getting choked up with emotion. It is quite a meaningful doctrine, isn't it?

Mark Christiansen

Mother in the Sky

∽

Mother in the sky
Your light shines in the trees
In every branch and leaf
Love, wisdom, and peace

Mother in the sky
Your light shines in the deep
Deep waters of my soul
You make me full

Mother
Mother in the sky
Goddess and Queen, divine
You bring light to my soul
Love to my heart
Wisdom to my mind

Mother in the sky
Your light shines in the night
In darkness shines the Moon
Showing me your might

Mother
Mother in the sky
Goddess and Queen, divine
You bring light to my soul
Love to my heart
Wisdom to my mind

Mother in the sky

    Eliza Freestone

Mind The Gap

As a father of two daughters, it is deeply hard for me to know how to talk to them about Heavenly Mother. I want them to understand that they have a divine archetype, but I am concerned that they will learn from the current cultural interpretation of Heavenly Mother that the ideal female is silent, submits to her husband's authority, lacks authority herself, and plays no visible role in the things that really matter.

I do not believe any of this is true about Heavenly Mother. After all, our doctrine explicitly teaches that She is equal to the Father in might and glory. But I wrestle as I encounter the gap between that glorious and unique truth and the reality of our often failing efforts to fully embrace it.

Taylor Webb

4

A Mother There

"In the heav'ns are parents single? / No, the thought makes reason stare; / Truth is reason—truth eternal / Tells me I've a mother there."

~ Mother in Heaven essay, paragraph 2

A Father and A Mother

I grew up
Seeking
Being taught
And learning to love
My Heavenly Father
The Eternal Father
Father of my spirit
He loves me,
A daughter of a King

And then
I see a quote
Here and there
About Mother

And then I start
To seek
To want to be taught
To learn to love
My Heavenly Mother

The Eternal Mother
Mother of my spirit
She loves me,
A daughter of a Queen

And now
I feel whole.

Lauren Robinson

Before She Was My Mother

what was She like
before She was my
Mother?

was She eager to start a family?
or was She nervous
knowing what was ahead of Her?

how did She and Father meet?
how did They decide how many children
to create?
how many worlds did They create
Together?

did She ever ask Him
why?
did They ever fight?

where did She go
when She needed time alone

to think about Her role
as Mother
Creator
Wife
Divine?

how many tears has She cried
over Her lost children,
Her resurrected Child?

who was She
before She was
my Mother?
before She had
Me?

Channing Olivia Hyde

Heavenly Mother's Name

My young daughter Evelyn knew Heavenly Mother's name. In fact, she thought she was named for Her. She prayed to her Heavenly Parents with every prayer.

We were saying "Father in Heaven," but she heard "Father and Evelyn."

Now you know.

Marci McPhee

In My Mother's Arms

Some serious health complications hit a few days before my daughter turned two, and I couldn't lift her for over a year. She was so patient and helpful, and when I finally healed, I lifted her out of a shopping cart one day without thinking about it. She was so surprised. In my arms, she exclaimed, "You can hold me!" and wrapped in the tightest hug and didn't want to let go. We stood there hugging in the parking lot, and it hit me how hard that had been on her, on both of us, for me to not be able to lift or carry her for the entire third year of her life.

At bedtime that night after prayer, she ran back into my room, folded her arms and said, "I forgot to say, Thank you that Mom can hold me. It took a REALLY long time. Amen."

The belief in Heavenly Mother is dear to my heart, and I sometimes feel like my daughter felt while I couldn't hold her—longing for closeness, trying to be big and strong. I picture myself saying something similar, if I could be held again. But then again, I do feel Her holding me. This drawing reminds me that I am in my Mother's arms, even when it feels like it's taking a REALLY long time.

Ashley Mansfield Hoth

Keep Going

When it was so dark and I was physically in so much pain that I couldn't get out of bed (that was only two days — but they were DARK days), it was Heavenly Mother and my absolute knowledge of Her at my spiritual level that kept me from throwing out all of the good things that I knew to be true.

Curt

Tell Julia

I was going through some difficult transitions and trials with moving, health issues, and a lack of joy.

I had been yearning for a greater connection with my Mother in Heaven for some time when the Relief Society President in my new ward left a voicemail. I didn't really want to talk and was heading out of town so I texted her that I didn't have time right now. She urged me to call when I got back, but I forgot.

The next Sunday she rushed to me as soon as sacrament meeting ended and gently held my arm. "Is your mother still alive?" she asked. When I told her Yes, she said, "Oh, then it wasn't her. I was awakened in the middle of the night to a calm, sweet, female voice that said: 'Please tell Julia that I love her and I'm here for her.'"

I believe that was my Mother in Heaven and that She spoke to me through my Relief Society President.

Julia B. Blake

Leaving for a Time

I left my baby for the first time
in the hands of others.
With a tear sliding down her cheek,
she uttered a quiet little cry as I left.

It was only for a short time—
but it felt so long.

When I returned
I said
I missed you.

I thought about you
the whole time.

Angela Ricks

A Memory

Despite our best efforts, sometimes we doze off while watching General Conference in our living rooms. I was between asleep and awake, and the conference speaker on the TV said something about the pre-mortal life that I heard just enough for a picture to shimmer into view in my mind — a path through a garden with beautiful flowers as large as my hands, in all colors. The sky was clear and blue with so much sunlight. Between the leaves of the trees, over there, was the golden-brown stone wall of a castle. I didn't see my Heavenly Parents, but I knew They were there inside. I was running with a friend toward it. We were happy and innocent, protected and loved. We were home.

I wonder if, when I pass from this world to the next, I will go back to that same garden and again run with my friend toward the castle where we will be happy, and loved, and home.

Trina Caudle

In Her Image: Ecuador

Anita Eralie Schley

In Dreams

In a dream
She came to me.
Or rather,
I ran to Her.
The back hall
In the church of my youth.
suddenly a holy place.

We embrace.
And falling to kneel
On the floor,
We weep.
"For this my daughter was lost, and is found."

When I wake,
One image remains.
Her robes.
Flowing with the elegant colors
Of a peacock's feather
And the shade of pink
from a newly rising sun.

Sadie Hanna

> "You sisters, I suppose, have read that poem which my sister composed years ago, and which is sung quite frequently now in our meetings. It tells us that we not only have a Father in 'that high and glorious place,' but that we have a Mother too; and you will become as great as your Mother, if you are faithful."

President Lorenzo Snow[11]

---

[11] *Teachings of Lorenzo Snow*, editor Clyde Williams, (Salt Lake City: Church of Jesus Christ of Latter-day Saint, 1998), 7.

A Mother's Touch

I walked with my first daughter midst life and knowledge grown
To teach her truth and wisdom and lessons never known.

I watched with anxious hoping as she took her first bite,
Then under blade aflaming, I said my last goodbye.

I sat there with the handmaid to calm her troubled heart,
Allay her casted thinking, her fears to all depart.

She could not see nor hear me; I reached inside her soul.
For soon she'd hold my baby, and we would share a role.

He stood in nurtured waters; I waited up above.
By Grace, entombed and risen, and I sent down a dove.

With still, small voice of whisper, I solemnly decreed:
This is my Son beloved, in whom I am well pleased.

I beckoned from the pages to come into the grove
The singing and the buzzing, his knees to them they drove.

Within the fire column, I hovered as the sun.
"Dear Joseph — My beloved; hear counsel from my Son."

Kim Siever

Mother of My Mothers

My mom and grandma are where memories of my earthly mothers end. Just two generations. Sleepovers with grandma, dancing in the street in our nightgowns before bed. Homemade bread for lunch that was more crust than bread, with a half-filled glass of Coke to wash it down. My mom's reckless laugh as she visited on the phone with friends, ministering before ministering was a thing. These women, these memories, helped form me into the woman I am today. Memories of my creation.

Both mothers have passed now and I'll admit, I feel a bit motherless. I yearn and reach for the influence of the mothers who help create me. I wonder, if I stretch far enough, if I reach past two generations into the eternal where creation and future join, can I reach the Mother of my mothers?

Karin Brown

She Is

Names on the trees: Mother God, Queen of Heaven, Wisdom, Elohim, Sophia, Asherah, Heavenly Mother, El Shaddai

Jennifer Alvi

A Mother Here

A Mother there? A Mother here.

I feel my Mother when I'm wrapped up in a blanket fresh out of the dryer.

I smell my Mother when the flowers bloom in Spring.

I see my Mother in the sunshine that breaks through the clouds.

I hear my Mother in the sound of leaves rustling and grass twirling in the wind.

My Mother is here. I can't wait to see Her there.

Alyssa Cranston

Trust

When I was finally brave enough to connect with my Mother in Heaven, to reach for my Mom, I learned to trust myself, find my voice, and trust my personal revelation. She taught me that I already knew Her and remembered Her and that I really do know who I am. I'm not crazy. Nothing is wrong with me. She taught me to honor my inner wisdom and respect myself.

Jill Freestone

Father, Mother, May I Meet You

Sometimes Prayer

Mom and Dad's door is open.
From the hall I see them in bed,
sitting up, faces flickering glory
and screenlight. Without a glance
away, they scoot a space
between themselves
to nestle me,
and we watch TV.

Kevin Kline

Mama, Mama

I watch my children play around me

Floating

It seems they barely touch the ground

Flitting from one second to the next

They are unaware of my sorrow

I sit

Weighed down like I am forged from lead

Too exhausted to move

Present, but far away

Lost in my thoughts and worries

The sound of my daughter's baby doll brings me back to the moment

"Mama, mama," it cries

And in my heart I echo its call

"Mama, Mama"

Alyssa Wilkinson

> "Think of the type of instruction you received in your pre-existent life as you were taught by your Heavenly Parents. Infinite People, Infinite Personages teaching you likewise to become infinite. And then They sent you here to receive this further instruction. It is a fact, brothers and sisters, that God watches over you and that you are here with a purpose in mind."

Elder Mark E. Petersen[12]

---

[12] Mark E. Petersen, "Be Ye an Exponent of Christ," Brigham Young University Speeches of the Year, 1965-1966 (Provo, Utah: Brigham Young University, 1966), 4, available online at speeches.byu.edu.

I Saw Her

I closed my eyes and saw Her,

Reaching out to me, beckoning,

Her eyes so kind and bright,

Her smile so warm,

She reaches Her arms high as the heavens

And wide as the earth

She shines like the sun

And dances wild in the night

She paints the stars in the sky

And holds them in Her hands

I am Her painted, created, beautiful star

She holds me in Her hand,

We reach high as the heavens,

And wide as the earth,

And we shine together,

We paint together,

And dance wild together.

Now I reach out to others, beckoning,

Come see Her, come feel Her,

Come reach with Her,

Come dance with Her,

Come paint with Her,

Come be one with Her.

Katie Freestone

The Yellow Brick Road

The scarecrow wished for a heart

The tin man longed for a brain

The Lion wanted some courage

And I thought I had to remain

Turns out You gave me a heart

And You also gave me a brain

Now they're pleading for courage

To reach You and find me again

Camilla Rodrigues

Opportunities to Seek

Professionally, I trained in Women's Health as an Obstetrician/gynecologist. My path through medical school, residency, and fellowship has provided the opportunity to listen to, advocate for, and serve women with diverse experiences and challenges. I am recognizing, more and more, my privilege, which is shaping the way I view myself and others.

During this journey, I feel I have received a generous response to my prayerful seeking to develop more charity. I wanted to share my experience to let you know that there are sons out there seeking and finding our Heavenly Mother as well!

Taylor Norton

Roots and Heavens

Today my mom and I
met up for an early
morning walk
along a lake shore.

My fearless dog pressed
her nose to tree roots,
as if she were making acquaintance
with holy ground.

We swapped stories —
traded bits of life, while
my hands ferociously
swatted dewy spider webs away.

"Let me go ahead"
My mom interrupted
my fruitless swipes at the air —
mouth spluttering.

"I've got a coat on,
and the webs won't get
on me. Let me
be your shield"

She said. "Oh
No," my voice
unenthused because
I really wanted her to.

And on we trudged —
her footsteps ahead,
paving the path
and catching the webs.

A clear path for me to follow
without getting tangled
in nature's fresh
morning strands

Meanwhile, tree roots twisted
and spilled over each other —
we scramble along,
eyes to the winding trail.

Glimpses of a glassy lake,
a mirror to the forest,
trees like arrows pointed
to the heavens.

Earthly mother.
Mother Earth.
Working in harmony to make
possible my exploration.

This poem is nonfiction, and when my mom offered to walk ahead of me to take the brunt of the early morning spider webs (we were the first morning hikers on this trail), I thought about a mother's love and sacrifice for her children. Mothers everywhere sacrifice their own comfort to better the position and opportunities of their children. It makes me think that our Heavenly Mother must have some iteration of that quality. I also loved the image of nature and motherhood intersecting in this moment — with Heavenly Mother represented in the tree roots and beauty of nature, I had both of my mothers present with me.

Erika Larsen

5

Side By Side

"Susa Young Gates, a prominent leader in the Church, wrote in 1920 that Joseph Smith's visions and teachings revealed the truth that 'the divine Mother, [is] side by side with the divine Father'."

~ Mother in Heaven essay, paragraph 3

In Tandem

I was earnestly seeking my Heavenly Mother on a sweltering August day two decades ago. For years already, I had struggled with the void of Her presence in my life, but on this occasion, my yearnings were particularly acute, maybe because I'd just given birth the week before.

I am intensely dedicated to my children, but when my first two children were born, I did not feel motherly joy or fulfillment I'd been promised my whole life. Even with precious, sacred experiences, my foray into motherhood left me raw and broken, inadequate, lost. Where was my Heavenly Mother to reassure me, guide me? I ached to know She was there and cared for me and loved me, along with the Father. I had long struggled with the void of Her presence in my life, but at the birth of my second child, the yearnings were acute. With prayers in our hearts for peace, comfort, and understanding, my husband and I traveled to the Nauvoo Temple, three hours from our home, our two-year-old and newborn in tow. Our plan was that my husband would stay with our little ones at the motel while I did an endowment session in the evening, and trade the next morning.

In the temple chapel, I immediately perked up when a male temple worker motioned to a woman standing at the end of our pew and instructed us to "follow the officiator." *Did he just call her an "officiator"?* I had never heard a woman referenced with this weighty title. I watched her very closely throughout the session, determined to understand why this designation was used and I noticed a pattern. She sat to the right of the man representing *Elohim*. Every time he stood, she stood. Every time he sat, she sat. All of their movements were in tandem. The Spirit impressed upon me that Heavenly Mother is at the right hand of Heavenly Father, jointly overseeing the instruction and teaching of Their children. Hidden in plain sight, She had always been right before my eyes. My heart flooded with profound peace and joy, and the Spirit witnessed the reality of Heavenly Mother's ever-presence and constant involvement in the lives of Her children with the Father. I held this tender, glorious manifestation in my heart for years, feeling strength and reassurance of my Mother's presence, awareness, and involvement.

I learned as an older adult that the Hebrew word *Elohim* is plural. Not long after learning that, I was reading *The Teachings of the Prophet Joseph Smith* and read with joy the following passage: "The word Elohim ought to be in the plural all the way through—

Gods."[13] The Spirit again affirmed what I discerned many years ago in the Nauvoo Temple, and witnessed anew that anywhere God the Father is, so is God the Mother. Their actions and engagement with Their children are never separate from one another.

Emily Spencer

---

[13] *Teachings of the Prophet Joseph Smith*, compiled by Joseph Fielding Smith, (Salt Lake City: Deseret Book, 1989), 372.

Equal

Equal in glory and majesty are our Father in Heaven and our Mother in Heaven. I testify that this doctrine is true.

Ashli Carnicelli

Partnership

Knowing that They were an equal team in Their plan for us helps my husband and I have a better partnership in our marriage. Knowing that They continue to work together for our salvation also helps me see Them as a team instead of Her silently watching the Father do all the work. I love being a team with my husband and love that that is the divine plan.

We often talk about Heavenly Father's love for us, but the Gospel Topics essay talks about how concerned both our Heavenly Parents are for us, that we are beloved by both of Them. What difference does it make to you to hear that She loves you and is daily concerned about you?

Jill Freestone

In Our Image

Elizabeth Bishop Wheatley

My Blessing

My patriarchal blessing tells me that my Mother in Heaven loves me and that spiritual gifts have come to me through Her. I was 15 when I received this blessing and I was lost in a myriad of questions and inner turmoil. This message was the most impactful knowledge I could have received at that time. It has defined my life in many ways. I am so grateful for loving Heavenly Parents that gave me this treasure in my time of need. I know this truth applies to all of us, we all are loved, we all have parts of our Heavenly Parents within us.

Mandi Lee Taylor

Involved

My husband Nate and I are very involved in the everyday things of our kids' lives. I know what special they have at school each day, their friends, their homework, their teachers, the kid in class that drives them crazy. I pray with them about recess plans as I shove them out the car door at school drop-off, and listen to the results at pickup. We scream embarrassing things at them at their cross-country meets and high-five at how hilarious we are. I know what our kids are nervous about, why their stomach hurts, and where their other shoe is hiding.

If this involvement is a badge of our love for our kids, how could the ultimate mother—Heavenly Mother—not be involved in our lives?

Gillian Smith

Equal Companions

I think one of the most important aspects of the doctrine of Mother in Heaven is that it helps to complete the doctrine of God and 'humanize' Heavenly Father. Even though we do believe in a God of 'parts and passions,' it is hard to conceptualize how Heavenly Father can be a perfect father without a matching companion who shares in this role. Without Heavenly Mother, it is much easier to see the title of Father as an abstract thing, an attempt to relate and impose our familiar structures on God.

With the doctrine of Heavenly Mother acknowledged, I find it easier to think of God not as an abstract being but as a partnership of two parents. Our families aren't just similar but following a pattern. Heavenly Mother, in some ways, also makes it easier for me to think about my relationship with Heavenly Father, even though how we think of fathers and what it is to be a Father is surely different.

Benjamin Bardsley

Lift Together

The world has tried to hand us a model that is unbalanced between men and women. Knowing my Heavenly Parents work "side-by-side" is the divine model I will follow.

What does this mean to me? I am a sovereign being married to another sovereign being and better things happen when we lift together. It may sound simple but it's actually very demanding to always show up and try.

I often fail ... but when I think of the model of my Heavenly Parents, I know I have to try again.

McArthur Krishna

When We Pray

Kayla Becknuss

Speakerphone

Whenever I call to catch up with my parents, who live far away, I must decide whether to dial my father's or my mother's phone number. Neither line is inherently better, but sometimes one is a more appropriate or convenient choice. Regardless, the parent who answers will invariably turn on speakerphone so the other parent can also hear and respond in the conversation.

I believe my earthly parents inherited this instinct from our Heavenly Parents, who are likewise eager to share a relationship with Their precious children. Though I figuratively dial Heavenly Father's number by addressing Him directly in prayer, I fully expect and envision that Heavenly Mother is likewise right by the metaphorical phone, participating in the entirety of Their heartfelt communication with me.?

Mikelle Lewis

A Wish for My Son

As a man in the Church, the doctrine of Heavenly Mother is important and cherished to me. I currently only have a young son, but I do want him to grow up in a world where women and men are treated equally, and I view the concept and doctrine of Heavenly Mother as an important way to help with that.

Tyler Sharp

Parents & Patterns

∼

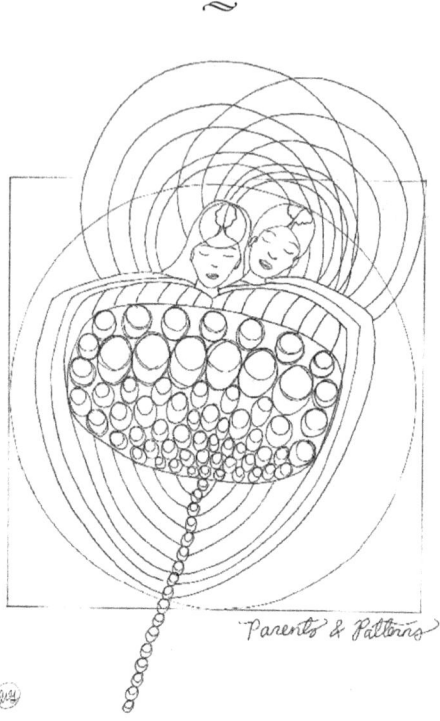

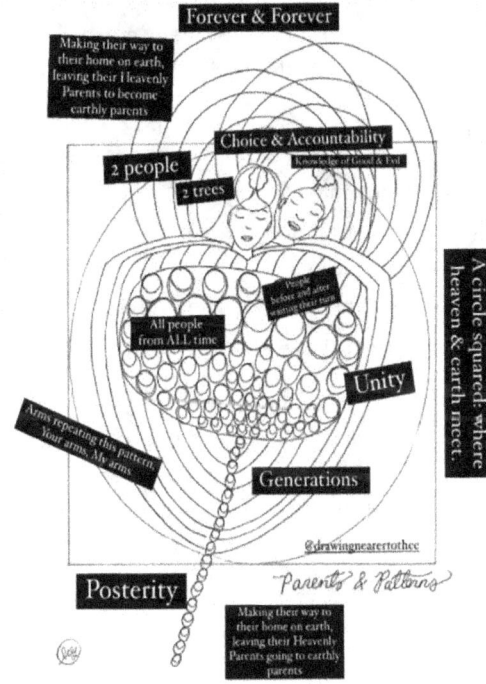

Michelle Gessell

Like the Little Drummer Boy

~

I don't write beautiful poems. I am not eloquent. I am loud. And try as I might, I often come across as brusque. All I can offer are my thoughts and truths.

We have a Heavenly Mother. She is as equal in might and power and glory as Heavenly Father. She is as full of love for us as He is. We often don't speak of Her due to cultural reasons, not doctrinal. But She exists.

I hope that once people realize that God is also She, they will see all the she's down here on earth as equal in value and as deserving of dignity as all the he's.

Darci Garcia

Plurality

We believe that "many great and important things pertaining to the kingdom of God" (Article of Faith 9) will be revealed in the last days. I'm certain that these things include knowledge of the Feminine Divine, and how She has been with us since the first days.

One place I see this is in the very name of God itself. "Elohim," like the angelic "cherubim" and "seraphim," is a plural word in Hebrew. Just as the latter words bring to mind "numberless concourses of angels" (Alma 36:22), the former has taken on a new meaning. Now, when I think of the Most High God, I see in my mind's eye a plurality, rather than a solitary figure.

Nathan Young

> "Miss [Eliza R.] Snow ... spoke on union, for us to simpathize one with the other, spoke of the pre exhistence of man, for us to live so that when whe leave this exhistence, we should return back to our Heavenly Parents."

Relief Society Minutes; Malad, Idaho, 1878[14]

---

[14] Relief Society minutes, May 5, 1878. Samaria Ward, Malad Idaho Stake. Original spelling. Relief Society Minutes and Records 1875-1973, volume 1, pages 34-35. Churchhistorianspress.org.

Long Before Our Time

~

Clara Packer, age 12

Creator

A few years ago, I was listening to a podcast while pulling weeds in the backyard. The woman being interviewed was talking about our Heavenly Parents and she said something about the Creation. As soon as the words came out of her mouth, it was like everything stopped around me. I didn't hear anything else she said. My mind had been opened to the beautiful truth that our Heavenly Mother had played a role in the Creation! Of course She did! It was like the entire gospel started falling into place and making sense to me. Our Mother has been there since the beginning. She knew us before we came to Earth. She helped design the beauty found in the palm fronds, Bird of Paradise flowers, tiger's stripes, my blue eyes, and my son's crooked smile.

Our Mother is a Creator! She is imaginative, artistic, whimsical, and visionary.

Anne Pimentel

Same Sociality

I don't know why the Father is mostly the only one spoken of at the general level. I don't think speaking of the Father is a bad thing at all, but I normally am left with a feeling of incompleteness, because I know that the same sociality that exists here is what exists in heaven — the Father doesn't act alone, but unitedly with our divine Mother. I regularly testify of our Heavenly Parents both at home and at church with confidence, for it feels like the most complete representation of my God.

Brother Heaps

In Her Image: Ethiopia

Anita Eralie Schley

United

It seems normal and natural to me that my Heavenly Mother would be as aware of me as my Father. They are the perfect parents, perfectly united in how They interact with Their children and what is best for us.

I've always assumed She was there, just more subtle. I see Her most through my Savior ... His kindness, compassion, gentleness, etc.

I believe She is one with my Father like my husband and I try to be united in all things.

Heidi Carey-Tasso

> "If we be the children of God; if it be true, as we have sung, and as I doubt not, that in the heavens parents are not single, but that we have a Mother as well as a Father there, then it follows that we, as the sons and daughters of God, bear within us the embryotic germs of Deity, and are capable by advancement, by progression, of becoming like our Father and our Mother in heaven."

Elder Orson F. Whitney[15]

---

[15] Orson F. Whitney, "Bishop O. F. Whitney," Woman's Exponent 24 (June 15, 1895): 9, contentdm.lib.byu.edu/digital/collection/WomansExp/id/32584/rec/540..

Interdependent

I'm engaged to be married and so excited to start a life with my fiancé! In our short time as an engaged couple preparing to be sealed, we have learned more than we could have expected about what it means to be half of a whole, part of a team—one functional unit.

One priceless lesson I have learned—and anticipate learning much more about in the future—is how interdependent we are on each other. Although we have different roles as husband and wife, father and mother, I feel that there's no way I could do whatever the Lord needs me to do without her. I just couldn't be who He needs me to be without her. In fact, I've never met an amazing stake president or mission president or relief society president who didn't have an equally amazing spouse with whom they were completely interdependent—with whom they were one. I wonder, then, if our Heavenly Father could be the Heavenly Father we know without a Heavenly Mother.

God, who has taught us the divine nature of an eternal companionship in which two people become one, surely practices the principles He teaches.

Ammon Hawkes

6

Divine Nature and Destiny

"In 'The Family: A Proclamation to the World,' issued in 1995, the First Presidency and Quorum of the Twelve Apostles declared, 'Each [person] is a beloved spirit son or daughter of heavenly parents, and, as such, each has a divine nature and destiny'."

~ Mother in Heaven essay, paragraph 3

Like Mother, Like Daughter

∽

My Mother, She loves me, I know this is true;
She birthed my existence, formed my spirit.
Creator of worlds, a Goddess Divine
Likewise I, in Her image, have an eternal destiny.

She birthed my existence, formed my spirit;
Concerned for my welfare, She's always watching.
I, in Her image, have an eternal destiny—In Her my eternal prototype lies.

Concerned for my welfare, She's always watching
My Mother knows me and is aware of me.
In Her my eternal prototype lies
I have potential to be a Goddess, like Her.

My Mother knows me and is aware of me;
She's constantly working to help me along.
I have potential to be a Goddess like Her,

A partner in a perfect union.
She's constantly working to help me along,
To bring to pass the immortality and eternal life of women.
A partner in a perfect union,
Her countenance, like His, radiates light.

To bring to pass the immortality and eternal life of women
Her work and glory is for my salvation.
Her countenance, like His, radiates light;
A woman of wisdom, Queen of Heaven.

Her work and glory is for my salvation
For I'm Her divine daughter, She's my eternal Mother;
A woman of wisdom, Queen of Heaven,
My Mother, She loves me, I know this is true!

Amelia Dunn

One Woman

What can one woman add to the conversation

I come with more questions than answers

I come with longings that will not cease

I want more

More Feminine Divine in my life

She has always been there

Even when it was too quiet

In the beginning there was light, Her bright light, Their light

During my earthly journey I have felt stirrings of Homesickness

I have a Mother whom I barely know

Yet I crave a connection with Her

She is there

It is my turn now for one woman to hold space for Her

Annie Packard Lewis

Welcome Balm

I think we have a long way to go in regard to how women are treated, but the doctrine of Heavenly Mother is a welcome balm.

Tyler Sharp

The Divine Feminine: Her Wisdom

Kiley Yates

I Want To Be Like Her

~

In a world of women

Where to "seem" is more important than to "be"

I want to "be."

I want to be like my Mother in Heaven

With Her endless depths of grace—

Of forgiveness

Of compassion

With Her arms open

Standing at the window of Heaven

Beside the Gate

Her shining heart beckoning us to Him—

Her Son,

I want to be

Kind

Patient

Long suffering

Full of goodness and truth and Light

Holy

Pure

Full of joy

Full of love

Ashli Carnicelli

Share Her Love

Last night, I laid in bed feeling really frustrated and sad. I was angry to live in a society where so many women are treated unfairly. On top of that, I was feverish, tight chested, and had a terrible sore throat. The pain inside me felt like it might burst open.

Suddenly, I had an overwhelming urge to feel my Heavenly Mother. I silently prayed to feel Her presence and immediately I felt Her surround me. Peace coursed through my body. I felt Her deep love for me. I could feel that our spirits are forever intertwined, that nothing can ever get in the way of my relationship with Her. She is a part of me and She is a part of all of the women around me.

I heard Her say, "You are blessed to be a part of a beautiful community of women in this church. Go serve and love these women and share My love for them." I heard Her say that She blessed me with four amazing daughters who are strong and loving. She urged me to help them remember their true selves, to help them connect to their spirits. She is a part of them too.

Then I sat and breathed. I asked Her to fill all the cells in my body with Her love. I felt Her ministering to my body. I could feel the areas that were sick being calmed and healed. I could breathe easy, when moments before my throat burned and my lungs were tight.

Then I laid and basked in Her love.

McKinzie Hancock

Female is Godly

We often only speak of Heavenly Father being the creator of our souls, but it took both Heavenly Parents. What difference does it make to you to know you have both a Heavenly Mother AND Father?

If I am made in the image of my Heavenly Mother and she is a Goddess, then my body, all my female parts are godly and like Hers. The world has a lot to say that denigrates or sexualizes women's bodies, but the female body is holy. Knowing whom I am made in the image of helps me be kind to my body and to love and accept it as it changes, stretches, aches, and seems to hormonally torment me, and especially through the Godly act of Mothering or all things related to being female. I was able to heal my troubled relationship with the female parts of me by more fully connecting with my Mother in Heaven.

Jill Freestone

> "Perhaps the most important things for us to see clearly are who God is and who we really are—sons and daughters of Heavenly Parents, with a divine nature and eternal destiny."

Sister Michelle D. Craig, counselor in Young Women general presidency, 2018-23[16]

---

[16] Michelle D. Craig, "Eyes To See," October 2020 general conference.

Queen

Megan Zabriskie Watson

Unique Blend

I have spent several months developing a personal relationship with the Divine Feminine. It would not be possible without the long process of "deprogramming" I've been going through regarding our culture of masculinity. As I've been able to accept the parts of myself that don't align with the proscriptive "manliness" I was raised with, I've found comfort that I can see those traits reflected in my understanding of the heavens.

As I am a child of Heavenly Parents, doesn't it stand to reason that I would inherit attributes from both? I come from two proud pioneer lineages (Hinckley and Young), and as I've grown, I've noticed what attributes and habits come from which side of the family. I can't imagine being uninterested in one just because the other lives closer, so why should it be any different with my Heavenly Mother? As there is a duality in most everything, there is a duality in me — my own personal goodness is a unique blend of two equal, eternal, but different goodnesses.

Nathan Young

Exploring

Giving myself permission to explore my relationship with my Heavenly Mother was like opening a hidden portal that had been there all along. I felt Her overwhelming presence on my walks, through the trees, in the air, the warm sun on my face. With no words, we had a conversation on a hike. I paused to look at a tree. The leaves had been at their peak and were now starting to fall. I felt Her everywhere in this grove of trees, but as I zoned in on one tree, words came to me about life and seasons and change. Constant reaching, growing, adapting, stretching towards source and light, enduring broken branches, loss, falling and starting new again, and again. Taking time to rest and be still, relishing the slowing down, the silence of winter, the thawing and new growth, new life, a fresh new palette. It was profound. My entire body felt as if it was vibrating. I stood there wishing I had a way to capture it all, to hold these pearls in my mind forever.

Andrea Weaver

A Child of Creation

I am out on a bike ride thinking about my family and Heavenly Mother. I was pedaling along a beautiful paved trail when I saw an incredible spider web. Something said, "Take a photo." I didn't. Pedaled another three miles and turned around and went back—to obey the Spirit and take a photo.

I parked my bike and knelt in the damp grasses to look more closely at the web. It was large, easily more than twelve inches in diameter. It was anchored by two thin strings on the left. More of a tangle of webs right of center. Another strand center bottom.

I crept closer and still closer, almost afraid my clumsy self may somehow undo this beautiful creation.

I looked everywhere for the spider who without a computer screen or artificial intelligence had somehow made this beautiful piece of art.

Even though I could not see the creator of the web, there was no question that the web existed and that it was magnificent in every way. As I watched the wind gently blow it, the web flexed and waved but the strands kept it secure in its format.

I thought about Heavenly Mother. I have never seen Her. I plan on meeting Her when I die. But I can look at myself, my spouse, my children and grandchildren, and all mankind and know beyond a shadow of a doubt that I am Her child. Her creation. I am a daughter of Heavenly Parents.

Kathleen McArthur

In Her Image: Germany

Anita Eralie Schley

Creating

"Creation flows from love. When we do what we love, we rejoice along the way." President Mary Ellen Smoot, Relief Society general president, 1997-2002.[17]

My mother-in-law and I shared a love of sewing and quilting. When she passed, I inherited her sewing machine, many colors of fabrics and threads, and a large plastic craft box of buttons lovingly sorted into colors.

Each time I sit down to sew, I think of her as I thoughtfully try to use at least a small portion of her supplies in my work. I have made quilts with her fabrics and clothing with her buttons or thread. I imagine she is happy when I use her gifts to create something beautiful. We are still sharing our love of working with fabric and thread.

Not only do I think of my mother-in-law when I begin a project, but of my Mother in Heaven, my creator.

---

[17] Mary Ellen Smoot, "We Are Creators," April 2000 general conference.

"We participate in the work of creation whenever we cultivate the earth or add our own constructions to the world. ... Our contributions may be expressed through the creation of works of art, architecture, music, literature, and culture, which embellish our planet, quiet our senses, and brighten our lives." Bishop Gérald Caussé, Presiding Bishop, 2015-current. [18]

Just as a button is useful and adds beauty to a garment, or as thread binds fabrics together and embellishes a quilt, I have practical and artistic gifts from my Heavenly Mother that help me when I create. I imagine She is happy when I use Her gifts to participate in the works of creation.

Lisa M. Foster

---

[18] Gérald Caussé, "Our Earthly Stewardship," October 2022 general conference.

> "Every one of us has been designed with a divine role and mission in mind. I believe that if our desires and works are directed toward what our Heavenly Parents have intended us to be, we will come to feel our part in Their plan. We will recognize the full measure of our creation, and nothing will give us more holy peace."

Sister Patricia Holland, counselor in Young Women general presidency, 1984-86[19]

---

[19] Patricia Holland, "Filling the Measure of Your Creation," BYU devotional, Provo UT, January 17, 1989.

Mother Maker

My Father is a Creator

My Mother, a Maker

She paints the sky pastels at the end of the day

Knits each one of us together by hand

Adding a special flourish to each one

Making us a masterpiece.

I see my hands and hope to be like Her

Innovative

Creative

Industrious

I hope my children look at me

And see their Mother Maker

Alyssa Wilkinson

Look At What I've Made

~

Hayley McBride

No Plan Without Her

A thought to ponder:

We talk about how there would be no plan without Jesus Christ, but the thought came that there would also be no plan without Heavenly Mother. She is the mother of our spirits, so She was required to put the plan in motion. The corollary is that there is no plan without women who are willing to give birth to and nurture children into this world.

Lisa Crawford

She Will Be There

As a little girl raised in the gospel, I knew what polygamy was. I did not understand the full implications of what that life could hold for women until I was a wife. As an adult, the idea of a woman only being a share holder to a loving spousal relationship was suddenly abhorrent to me. I don't know what brought this concern on, but I felt a need to know if polygamy would be practiced in the holy spaces of God. I felt like the promise of eternal joy was falling from my grasp and it was heart wrenching.

I scoured gospel libraries for anything about eternal marriage. I cried, a lot, for days. My husband did not understand the depth of my emotions over this. I only found talks on the subject from men. I didn't feel confident approaching any women I knew with such a delicate topic. I could not find solid answers, so there was no recourse to temper my sorrow but prayer.

As I prayed, I felt I needed to seek the words of women who had lived polygamy in mortality, and I took an interest in Eliza R. Snow. One day, I read the hymn lyrics of "O My Father" which she wrote—the line "I've a Mother there" sank deep into my person.

I knew the truth of that statement and felt the love and presence of my Mother. Someday She would explain everything I did not yet understand. That was enough for my spirit to know, and it was a turning point in my faith.

Josie Ann Grover

I Wonder If We Knew

I wonder if we knew that missing Her would be so hard,

I wonder if for a moment we saw what this life would be like,

and if we questioned whether we'd come.

I wonder if we tarried, asking for just a little more time,

to be held, to memorize Her face.

I wonder it we knew ...

That our knowledge and understanding of Her

would be so wiped clean away,

I wonder if we knew that our path back to Her

would be so foggy and unclear.

I wonder if we knew …

That we might get lost along the way.

I wonder if we knew that our hearts

would hold the map that would lead us back home.

I wonder if we knew …

that missing Her so deeply

would help us seek Her more earnestly.

I wonder if we knew …

that the journey would change us so,

I wonder if we knew …

And chose the path of life!

I wonder if we knew that remembering Her would feel like home.

As my spiritual eyes are opened,

As my vision begins to clear,

As my spirit begins to remember,

I no longer need to wonder,

I think we knew ...

    Tammy Zufelt Thomas

Things Hoped For –
She Discovers Heavenly Mother's Likeness In Herself

~

Emily Carruth Fuller

The Young Women Values

We believe in Heavenly Father and Heavenly Mother—Faith.

We are Their children—Divine Nature,

and can become like Them in eternity—Individual Worth.

As we learn and grow—Knowledge,

we make better choices and take responsibility for our actions—Choice and Accountability.

Our choices include extending service and sharing our Heavenly Parents' love—Good Works.

What we do when no one is watching—Integrity,

determines the direction of our lives—Virtue.

Trina Caudle

7

Work Together

"Prophets have taught that our heavenly parents work together for the salvation of the human family."

~ Mother in Heaven essay, paragraph 4

A Day With the Gods

~

He rests in cathedrals.
She rests among the aspen trees.
They meet at the farmer's market, hold hands,
and make up words for the tunes that float
from a squeaky violin.

She sits upon a shining throne.
He sits down in a beanbag chair.
They share a chuckle when the organist plays
at half tempo
yet again.

He loves the spring.
She loves the chilly fall.
They watch reruns of the World Cup, pass the chips,
and cheer for different teams.

She tends to the night owls.
He tends to the many-colored early birds.

For lunch They make
peanut butter sandwiches
and cut them diagonally.

Nathan Young

The Doctor's Wife

My husband is a heart failure/heart transplant cardiologist. He attended medical school, did an internal medicine residency, did a cardiology and heart failure fellowship, and obtained the knowledge, education, and skills required to perform his duties and provide care as a physician.

Yet when he goes to work, his patients receive care from both of us in a team effort. First, I labored beside him to provide the means necessary for him to complete his education and be able to care for his patients as he does today. Second, I labor beside him still, praying for him and his patients every day. I am so grateful for the many ways the Spirit has prompted me to pray for him in his work and I know that this makes a difference.

One morning during my prayers, I felt a clear prompting to pray about a specific procedure that he needed to perform on a patient, a cardiac catheterization. I do not know details about the patient due to privacy, but the Spirit was firm — "Tony and his patient need your extra prayers today." I was obedient. At the end of the day my husband came home, his face very drawn and tired. "Today was the hardest case I've ever had in the cath lab. But my patient is going to be okay." I told him what the Spirit had prompted me and he wus grateful, yet not surprised at all.

This has made me wonder how many miracles and tender mercies have come as a result of both of our Heavenly Parents working together for our good. I wonder how both of Their efforts, seen and unseen, fit together in perfect harmony to make the outpouring of Their love possible in our lives.

Ashli Carnicelli

Dance of the Creators

J. Kirk Richards

Divine Model

Northwestern University[20] recently released the summary of their findings after analyzing 6 million studies. What they discovered?

Projects trying to solve complex problems that had an equal (or almost equal) number of men and women on the team ALWAYS outperformed other team configurations. And it makes perfect sense—the model of equal representation between men and women follows the divine pattern of heaven that says our Heavenly Parents "work together" for the salvation of Their children. Working together as equals has the best chance of solving problems.

McArthur Krishna

---

[20] Max Witynski, "What happens when women and men work together?" Northwestern Now, August 29, 2022, news.northwestern.edu/stories/2022/08/gender-balanced-teams-produce-more-innovative-impactful-scientific-research/.

Advice & Comfort

I hold my earthly mother's hand

And listen to the rhythmic tones of the many machines

Monitoring her life force

With every new chime I hold my breath

What does it mean?

In the quiet moments

Between nurses bustling

And doctors discussing

I find myself seeking

Reaching

Looking to my Father for advice

And to my Mother for comfort

Alyssa Wilkinson

Undivorcing: A Letter

Dear Mother,

Matthew 19:6 says, "Wherefore they are no more twain, but one flesh. What therefore God hath joined together, let not man put asunder."

There is no couple more joined together by God than ... well, God. Someday I hope You'll tell me how You and Father came together. Was Your marriage arranged? Did You meet and fall in love? Have You simply always been One?

However it happened, You are One now.

I was just thinking about a conversation I had with my sister about the painting *In Their Image* by Caitlin Connolly — she said seeing it "undivorced" You from Father in her mind. The word rang around like a loose bell in my chest.

Your children have divorced You. We have put You asunder. We have even feared pitting

You against each other and making Father jealous of our love for You like there's some kind of heavenly custody battle.

You and Father are Love. I wonder if it hurts You both when Your children ignore Your divine marriage. I can imagine my joyful Father wincing a little when a beloved child comes unto Him ... but doesn't see You at His side. I know it would break my heart if my son didn't have a relationship with my husband.

I'm learning to think of You as a couple in love and to use Your example in my marriage. I try to speak of You together whenever I can. And I look forward to returning to Your joint presence someday.

"What therefore God hath joined together, let not man put asunder."

Love, Marnae

Marnae Kelley

Embrace of Divine Harmony

In the celestial tapestry, where stars sing silently, there stands a Supreme Couple, Heavenly Father and Mother, equal and ever-united, embodying the essence of infinite equilibrium. Their presence portrays the perfect partnership.

They are the Cosmic Creators, crafting constellations and galaxies with gentle grace, guiding galaxies, gently governing the grandeur of the universe. Their hands, harmonious and hallowed, hold the heartbeat of existence, forging futures and fostering flourishing life.

In Their unity, there's an unstoppable undercurrent of undying love, where masculine and feminine forces find fertile ground for flourishing. They are the paragons of partnership, teaching that strength is not in separation but in symbiosis, and power is not in hierarchy but in harmony.

Heavenly Father and Mother, a divine duet, dance in the dimensions beyond human discernment. Their song, sweet and subtle, serenades the cosmos, soothing the soul and stirring the spirit, as They share secrets of the celestial symphony.

In Their unity, we uncover the ultimate understanding of the divine, where duality and distinction merge into the magnificent mosaic of oneness. Their equal existence ignites the imagination, awakening awe, and ascending aspirations.

As we aspire to absorb Their essence, we acknowledge Their alchemical artistry, transforming trials into triumphs, and turbulence into transcendence. In Their unity, the universe unfolds its unparalleled potential, proving that partnership, predicated on loving principles, is the pinnacle of power.

Heavenly Father and Mother, in Their eternal embrace, illuminate the path to enlightenment and equality, encouraging every entity to embrace their essence, embrace each other, and embark on an expedition towards an existence where equality and equilibrium reign supreme.

Guillermo Lemus

In Her Image: Ghana

Anita Eralie Schley

Role Models

There is a lot of talk about women needing a role model and men having their role model. I argue that we all need both role models.

To become a Man, I need to learn from the divine yin-yang that is my Heavenly Parents. For my wife to become a Woman, she needs the same. We cannot reach our full individual potential learning just from our Father.

I just want it understood that we boys are also missing out. Human development psychologists tell us that boys learn important lessons about being boys from their mothers, and girls learn important lessons about being girls from their fathers. Do we expect anything different in the Heavenly model? I need and want my Mom as much as anyone!

Karl Hale

> "Will you join me in seeking the help of the Holy Ghost to teach us how we can better lift each other ... as covenant sons and daughters of our loving Heavenly Parents?"

President Linda K. Burton, Relief Society general president, 2012-17[21]

---

[21] Linda K. Burton, "We'll Ascend Together," April 2015 general conference.

Mother, May I?

Mother, may I ask You something?

If Father God weeps, do You weep also?

When You see Your children fighting

And wars waging

And hearts growing cold?

Or does Your Mother heart

See past the actions

And look at the heart

Of Your divinely known

And deeply loved offspring?

Sarah Waddoups

They Saw It Was Good

~

Hannah Milmont McCort

Resonate

As a man seeking to understand the character of a Heavenly Father, to then try to understand the character of a Heavenly Mother when I can't even understand a mortal woman is a bit daunting. However, this doctrine resonates with me because I want my wife-mother standing co-equal together with me in the eternities.

Brent A. Fisher

Finding Mother in Song

Sally DeFord has written a Christmas song entitled "Guard Him, Joseph" that honors the earthly father of Jesus Christ and the role he played. As my husband and I prepared the duet version for our Christmas program, I pondered on this piece and possible interpretations.

As a singer, I am trained to consider who the speaker of each song is, even if it is not explicitly stated. In this particular arrangement, I sing one verse, and my husband sings the next before we sing together.

As I pondered this song, I wondered if perhaps the speakers could be Heavenly Mother and Heavenly Father. It brings peace to my soul to imagine loving Heavenly Parents excitedly watching the birth of Christ. They understand the magnitude of this moment, and They are filled with so much love.

Now, I love singing it and seeing Heavenly Mother and Heavenly Father giving Joseph the courage and strength to take on the role he was given.

If Heavenly Mother and Heavenly Father were to sing a song to you, what would it be? What message would They want to share?

Malinda Wagstaff Metro

The Bleed

I was 13, and I started to bleed.

My heart wasn't ready to let go,

    Weeping for a childhood's winter.

My father loved me,

Yet he was unknowing.

He loved me and looked to my mother.

She gave me aspirin, wrapped me in a warm compress,

and let me cry in my bed.

I am 28, and my womb won't stop bleeding.

My heart won't stop aching,

    Beating an open wounded song.

My Father loves me,

And He is all-knowing.

To love me, He looks to my Mother.

She holds me, giving me love, wrapping me in light,

    Letting me cry in my bed.

Charlotte Wilson

Prepared For Such A Thing

Every child ushered in
Prepared for such a thing

A Heavenly Parents blessing
Inseparably connected

Every birth
the veil between
Heaven & Earth
thinning

The unseen scene of Them attending

A newborn cry
A celebration for parents here
Letting go of Parents there
A newborn tear singing

Borrowed time
Glimmers
Reassuring
Spiritual beings ringing

A thrill of anticipation
A newborn King
A newborn you

A Family Union

Every nation
Every knee

Sacrifice
Salvation
Journey
Human experience bringing

Prepared for such a thing
Eternal reunion
Sealing

Michelle Gessell

The Rest in the Symphony

From my balcony seat in a beautiful concert hall several years ago, I marveled as a symphony orchestra played a captivating rendition of Beethoven's Fifth Symphony. To my bewilderment, however, the orchestra appeared to be a beat behind the conductor every time they played the famous "da-da-da-dum" sequence.

My mother, an accomplished violist, later explained to me quite simply what I misunderstood: the first beat in the measure was a rest.

I had naively assumed that the familiar segment began on the downbeat of each measure. Until I literally saw the symphony and the rest performed, and my mother resolved the seeming discrepancy, I didn't realize my perception of the musical score was inaccurate.

Combining rests with musical notes is essential

for a coherent and harmonious piece.

Similarly, prophets have taught that our Heavenly Parents work together for the salvation of the human family. Although we may be more conscious of our Heavenly Father's role in Their plan, Heavenly Mother's role is in every respect equally integral in the symphony that is Their glorious work.

Can we learn to recognize Her as clearly as the rests between familiar notes?

Mikelle Lewis

> "Come to me; here's the mystery that man hath not seen:
> Here's our Father in heaven, and Mother, the Queen,
> Here are worlds that have been, and the worlds yet to be:
> Here's eternity, —endless; amen."

W.W. Phelps[22]

---

[22] W. W. Phelps, "Come to Me," in "Poetry, for the Times and Seasons," *Times and Seasons* 6 (Jan. 15, 1845): 783.

Understanding Marriage

It's exciting to think about how much more my marriage (and everyone else's) would be enhanced by better understanding the role of Heavenly Mother in The Archetypal Eternal Marriage.

Chris Slemp

8

Designers of the Divine Plan

"'We are part of a divine plan designed by Heavenly Parents who love us,' taught Elder M. Russell Ballard of the Quorum of the Twelve Apostles."

~ Mother in Heaven essay, paragraph 4

Divine Design: The Spiritual Creation

~

In the books of Abraham and Moses, we learn the marvelous truths that the heavens and the earth were created spiritually before they were created naturally. (Abraham 5:5)

I can see Heavenly Father's omnipotent hand in the spiritual design:

Of the majestic mountains.

The rushing rivers.

The deepest oceans.

The tallest redwoods.

The great whales.

The intensity of the sun.

And in the torrential rains.

And I see Heavenly Mother's powerful but gentle hand in the spiritual design:

Of the snow and evergreens on the winter mountain peaks.

In the graceful waterfalls along the flowing rivers.

In the curling waves on the white sandy shores of the beautiful blue ocean.

In the song of the mama whale calling to her calf.

In the blushing leaves of the fall trees.

In the endless variety of flowers blooming in the spring meadows.

In the stunning changing sunsets of summer.

In the lyrical melodies and harmonies of the most uplifting music.

In the inspiration of great art.

In the most graceful deer and the softest angora rabbit.

In the shining moon and twinkling stars against the dark night sky.

And after the torrent,

In the vibrant colors of the rainbow.

But I see both of Their loving hands in the creation of adorable babies, innocent children, and upright and honest mature adult men and women made in Their individual images.

Her sorrow for the sins of Her children must be great. But I can feel Her eternal compassion in the sacrifice of Her Firstborn Son on our behalf. And I can hear Her loving words in His Gospel.

So, it could follow ...

In the very beginning the Gods, Heavenly Father and Heavenly Mother, spiritually created the heavens and the earth ...

S. Douglas Phillips

Heavenly Mother

Emily Carruth Fuller

Blood and Sap

With tenderness,

Mother catalogues and curates

trillions of moments,

the details stored in Her branches-

branches that endlessly grow and reach,

new leaves unfurling, taking note:

the little tomboy who loves the smell of vanilla,

la gitana who spent hours on the blue skirt for her daughter,

the boy with smeared eyeliner singing his heart out,

and all the names

(She loves names, loves naming things),

our names,

embedded in the flesh of the heartwood,

memories stored in Her roots,

keeping them safe,

tucked warm into the soil.

Megan Thompson

A Woman's Touch

I've often heard
That a house becomes a home
With a woman's touch
To me that rings true
For this world of ours

I see my Father in the construction
The planning
The golden ratios repeated so perfectly
Organized
Logical
Precise

I see my Mother in the embellishment
The beauty
The sprinkles of color and whimsy
Playful
Joyous
Free

Alyssa Wilkinson

A Christmas Anthem to Heavenly Father & Heavenly Mother

Oh Father and Mother, I thank Thee

For thy Son,

Thy Firstborn Son of the Morning!

The rightful heir of all,

Thy perfect creation.

Thou didst love Him perfectly,

And thus He learned to love.

And when Thou didst ask for a Savior,

He loved enough to give His life for me.

Hallelujah!

The stable called, and He descended to mortality.

Mary and Joseph had Thy trust.

With them, Thou didst rejoice as Jesus

Walked and talked and learned and loved—
for the second time.

He went about doing good, and He lived a sinless life.

The pure in heart recognized; they followed.

And when the time did come to descend yet again,

He confirmed His choice to save us all.

"Thy will be done."

Hallelujah!

The crushing sorrow and sin of His seed

Burst His heart in Gethsemane, and then

Betrayal and stripes, kingly crown and royal robe,

And finally, cross and spikes and spear for me.

Despite the injustice and Thy pain, Thou didst not intervene.

The tomb tenderly, gently received the Creator,

The imprisoned spirits got the keys to the locks,

And the resurrection miracle began.

Hallelujah!

He came to earth, Oh Glorious Gift from Heaven.

We thank Thee Mother! We thank Thee Father!

We thank Thee Jesus, Oh Wondrous Gift from Heaven.

Hallelujah!

Steven R. Theobald

In Her Hands

Rebecca Frailey

> "We are taught that men and women, the sons and daughters of God, who were spirits in His presence, were sent here to take mortal tabernacles and undergo experiences that would in due time exalt them to the plane occupied by their Father and Mother in heaven."

Elder Orson F. Whitney[23]

---

[23] "The Apocalypse," *Collected Discourses* 1886-1898, vol. 5, edited by Brian H. Stuy, (Woodland Hills, Utah: BHS Publishing, 1999).

Four Births

A Mother strong had birthed that day the sun, the moon, and stars.
She placed each one upon the sky—the night and day apart.
The waters from within Her womb now baptized all the earth
With rivers, oceans, lakes, and streams, all products of that birth.

Another day, the Mother bore all seeds of every kind,
Then planted them in soil enriched by water, blood entwined.
Each seed grew up so mighty, strong, warmed by the sun above,
And flowered, fruited, bounty grew, nourished by Mother's love.

On the third day, from Mother dear, came fin, and wing, and paw.

"It is good," our Mother said, as She looked out and saw
The measure of creation made, each type and, too, each kind.
"But even 'mong my children here, there're some I do not find."

So on day four, She birthed once more, and out came those like Her:
Her beauty, strength, persistence, brains, and meekness, courage sure.
Her creation now complete, She drew Her children near:
The beasts, the fowl, the fish, the plants, the humans—Her whole sphere.

She counselled them, "You all are one, through birth, and life, and death.
You take, you give, you show respect, in appetite and breath."

And then She spoke specifically to those who She'd birthed last.
"Because you look and act like Me, the torch to you I pass.

"To you the role of gardener, to nurture and to grow,
"To you the role of shepherd, too, each beast and bird to know.
"To you the keeper of the sea, to keep it full of life.
"To you protector of the sky, the source of breath and light."

Concluding now Her court divine, She shared a sacred truth,
"Your death is not the end for you; for yours' a godly youth.
"Just as I planted seed on earth, I planted seed in you,

"A seed that grows with trial and curse, and wisdom, pow'r its fruit.

"The roots that grow within your heart will reach up toward Me.
"The branches stretching out in faith, embrace eternity.
"Divinity is in your past, your future it entwines,
"For you, My children, each of you, is naturally divine."

Kim Siever

In Her Image: Guatemala

Anita Eralie Schley

It Can Be AND

I'm currently taking the huge climb back into full time employment. I stayed home with my babies for 14 years. It was what I thought I wanted. It was the default, the expected thing. It was hard and isolating, and sacred work and lovely. But working during that time felt impossible. Restarting a career with so much time lost was daunting.

When my youngest entered first grade, the pressure to work was suddenly coming from everywhere. I was angry and hurt at the suggestion and lost at how to even re-enter the work force. My degree was old, my certifications had lapsed. The battle raged in my mind almost constantly.

One morning, I got personal direction from Heavenly Mother. I was lying in bed on a weekend morning, listening to the most delicious summer rainstorm, wrapped in a fluffy blanket, the most relaxed I'd been in a long time. I heard a distinct voice:

"I can make babies AND send rain."

The rain is my favorite summer weather. It's comforting, soothing, nourishes the earth. It's also powerful, destructive, and necessary for change and growth. My role as mother is important, AND I can do more with my time that can influence others in powerful ways and use my talents to be like my Heavenly Mother.

It doesn't have to be either/or ... it can be AND.

Marci Petersen

Luna

Brushing clouds smear charcoal skies
Her steady hands grow heavy
Our world shakes as day blinks eyes
She settles down for nightly cries

Every drop of mourning flood
Kindles breath and eases blood
A nameless love—while
Release and grief bring sweet relief

Her weepings cease
As surely will our infamy,
each enmity,
And every grave forsaken

Now heavens gaze from lunar rays
While we solely stand
Tributing the sun

Emotion's found in careless breeze

Parental passion hardly seen
She co-creates eternity
Though is She—unknown to me

Zachary Brady

Our Heavenly Mother

April Sorbonne

> "All of us commenced a wonderful and essential journey when we left the spirit world and entered this often-challenging stage called mortality. The primary purposes of our existence upon the earth are to obtain a body of flesh and bones, to gain experience that could come only through separation from our Heavenly Parents, and to see if we would keep the commandments."

President Thomas S. Monson[24]

---

[24] Thomas S. Monson, "Ponder the Path of Thy Feet," October 2014 general conference.

Mother Editor

~

The Word
Weaves, paints, creates
A world without form, spoken into existence

The Editor, thoughtful and organized
Grants a nurturing foundation
Polishing beauty to splendor
Chaos to art
As a womb
Clarifying intention to perfection
Quiet and powerful
Working unseen to the untrained eye
A heartbeat heard only by those close enough to listen
She too, speaks
And Her child, author and perfecter
Is taught at Her knee

Without the Editor, the Word would not be
But because of She—
"I Am."

Jessica Vergara

A Place In My Heart

My life changed when I gained a Heavenly Mother.

Since I was young, I understood that I have a Heavenly Mother in the same way I have a Heavenly Father. However, like many doctrines of the restored gospel of the Church of Jesus Christ, this understanding was on a cognitive level and bore no weight in my quotidian life.

It wasn't until I was in my twenties that I understood in my heart that I am a son of a Heavenly Mother and allocated attention to this truth so that it could impact the way I see myself and those around me.

The doctrine of Heavenly Mother is dear to me because when it gained a place in my heart, I truly saw the parental nature of God. I had addressed God as Heavenly Father for so many years, yet He lacked His "fatherliness" until I could instinctively pair Him with His counterpart—a Mother.

These days, all of my beliefs are put through a lens that every person on earth is a child of Heavenly Parents. This reframing has had massive and beautiful implications.

Nathan T. Glade

Pure Light

Throughout the ages and across religious traditions, Divine beings have been described using words relating to light: bright, lightning, fire, sun, radiant, gleam. It makes sense to me that divinity would appear light rather than any shade or tint of color. It took me a while to differentiate between the two.

If you take a set of rainbow colored paints and mix them together, you'll get some variant of brown or black. However, when you mix all the colors of the rainbow together in *light*, it creates pure white light. This is because the paints mixing together is a *subtractive* process and light is an *additive* process. A being of pure light cannot exist without every color in the rainbow; because light is expansive and additive, not subtractive.

And don't you think our Mother wants all the

many colors home as well? The reds, yellows, blues, and everything in between? This piece is not a perfect vision of what lives in my head. But it's the closest I can get for now.

Jaida Brown Hancock

Divine Matryoshka Doll Line

"All the eggs a woman will ever carry form in her ovaries while she is a four-month-old fetus in the womb of her mother. This means our cellular life as an egg begins in the womb of our grandmother. Each of us spent five months in our grandmother's womb, and she in turn formed within the womb of her grandmother. We vibrate to the rhythms of our mother's blood before she herself is born, and this pulse is the thread of blood that runs all the way back through the grandmothers to the first mother."[25]

Once while contemplating my Mother in Heaven

Considering how we are connected

How we are alike

---

[25] Layne Redmond, When The Drummers Were Women: A Spiritual History of Rhythm, (Brattleboro, Vermont: Echo Point Books & Media, 2018).

I saw myself in the middle of a line of noble women

I saw myself as the middle Matryoshka Doll

I was carried in my mother's womb

And in my grandmother's womb I was also carried

My grandmother was in her grandmother's womb

From womb to womb along my matriarchal line

My Mother In Heaven carried me and all of my mothers

She holds me and wraps Her arms around me

Just like She held all my mothers

Carrying us through all the heaviness

I love feeling this connected to all the noble women in my line back to my Mother God

Knowing and feeling our hearts and bodies are interwoven and held together

I see us all inside each other

Sharing so many aspects of ourselves

Sharing divine attributes directly from Heavenly Mother

Knowing this and connecting with all the women in my line helps me love and respect each of us in the ways we are both alike and different

Just as I carried and birthed my daughters

And then hold them in their times of need

I place myself in each of my mothers arms

physically, mentally, and spiritually

And let us all carry and hold

Each other tight

Bound together through our

Divine Matryoshka Doll line.

Jill Freestone

Light and Life

∾

While wandering among the aspen trees on a fall morning, I looked up and saw, as if my eyes were open to the things of the Spirit, every leaf glimmering with the light that "is in all things, which giveth life to all things" (D&C 88:13).

The phrase "Mother Earth" came to mind, and I also remembered that the Mother of the Son of God was seen in connection with the interpretation of the tree of life (1 Nephi 11: 18).

For a moment I was filled with the love that is inherent in creating life out of mortal matter, infused with eternal spirit. I felt a profound love for my Heavenly Parents who have created this life, infused with Their spirit, where I can learn to love as They do.

Craig Merrill

I'm Finding Her

I'm finding Her in autumn
In the process of creation
That begins with death
a necessary step
Towards a joyful rebirth
I'm finding Her in rivers –
The destructive force
Of water
Clearing a path,
Making way for the new
I'm finding Her in stars,
hidden diamonds that
show themselves
only to those who
venture into the darkness
I'm finding Her in lilac
a pleasant purple hue:
gentle and soft,
delicate but strong
maternal, and kind
I find Her somewhere new every day, but
only if I watch, and listen

Danielle Kemp Nelson

Gifts from Mother God

∽

Hey Mother
It's me, Your daughter.
I love You.
I miss You.

Hey Mother
I've been thinking
Of the gifts I've been given
From you.

You gave me a smile
That welcomes others in
And shows them they're safe
And loved.

You gave me a sixth sense.
The ability to tell
When others are struggling
And need someone to talk to or be with.

You gave me Your ears
And You gave me Your heart
To listen to others
And love them, and validate them.

You gave me Your arms
To embrace Your children
To take them in when they need help
And be a vessel through which they can feel
Your love.

You and Father gave me the gift
To call upon You in times of need.
What an incredible gift
That I need to develop and use more often.

Mother, I'm humbled
That you trust me with these
That others can feel You and Father
Through me.

Mother I'm so imperfect
And I lose my way often
Yet You entrust me with these gifts
Regardless.

Mother, help me
To be worthy enough
To emanate Your love
To those I interact with.

Hey Mother
It's me, Your daughter.
I love You.
I miss You.

Mother,
Make me more worthy of Your love
So I can be the vessel
Through which others feel it.

Emily Felt

9

Influences from Beyond

"President Harold B. Lee stated, 'We forget that we have a *Heavenly Father* and a *Heavenly Mother* who are *even more concerned*, probably, than our earthly father and mother, and that *influences from beyond* are constantly working to try to *help* us when we do all we can.'"

~ Mother in Heaven essay, paragraph 4

Stop and Feel the Flowers

~

I watched you touch the wheat grass, and smell the forget-me-not.

Everything that was eye level at two.

I felt how fleeting that sweet little slow-down would come to be.

There's a Mother watching me watch you, growing the forget-me-nots.

Showing me everything at eye level in my mothering years.

She knows how fleeting my time away will come to be.

She knows some days feel much longer in my heart.

She sends forget-me-nots.

Maddie Daetwyler

She Taught Me To Love

She is everywhere. She is IN me, just as I am part of my mother and grandmother and part of my daughters. Knowing my Heavenly Mother changes everything. I know who I am and who is with me and what my potential is.

She taught me to embody complete love for myself and for others. She taught me to love my physical body, with its powerful tiger stretch marks, laugh lines, wisdom wrinkles, and silver highlights in my hair. She taught me to love my quirks, my often painful black-and-white brain, my chronic pains, my emotional and physical sensitivity, my anxiety, depression, and OCD, my sickness and irritable bowel, my sagging breasts, my squishy stomach and thighs. She taught me to love ALL of me, because I am divine as a woman, a daughter of a Goddess.

By connecting with and knowing my Mother

in Heaven, I was able to heal my troubled relationship with the female parts of me: my period, my pregnancies, births, and nursing and hormone complications.

For most of my life, I felt Heavenly Father and Jesus's love and presence and that was powerful. But the completeness of knowing my Mother as well is almost indescribable until you experience it.

We all need our Mother, not just women. There are many times when I need my father and other times when I need my mother and also many times I need my Savior Jesus Christ. This completes me. I am whole.

Jill Freestone

Four Trees

Once there was an orchard small of four trees in a row.
Planted by a gardener, from seedlings She did grow.
Nurtured, pruned, and shepherded, a sight now to behold,
Underneath their branches wide, four stories did unfold.

Fruit upon the first was dark and light and soursweet.
Life bestowed for years on end till children wisdom eat.
Blossomed mind but death inside with flame and blade depart.
Memories are buried deep, replaced by broken heart.

Second tree bore bitter fruit, a painful, bloody red.

Nurtured by the root of kings through weighted vine and bread.
Gardener in garden dark donating strength to will,
Straightening the woollen back, the harder coming still.

Third tree bare, stripped of its leaves, its shadow growing more,
Howling winds and lightning flash along with thunder's roar.
Piercing fruit falls to the ground, causing trembling quake.
Friends and family, followers, and everyone forsake.

Honey fruit on number four was beck'ning from the page,
Turning keys within the locks to free the prayers from cage.

Once again, the Gardener loomed, but this time all ablaze.
With a motion of Her hand, She opened heaven's rays.

Kim Siever

The Mother and Her Sisters

∽

Chelsea Echols

Heavenly Mother at 2000 Feet

My husband and I traveled to Italy for a vacation and left our four daughters in the capable hands of both our parents. I felt very anxious to go without them.

The Spirit nudged me and said, "Heavenly Mother will reveal Her face to you in Italy —you need to go."

From the moment we arrived at our first destination on the Amalfi Coast, I could feel Her powerful love. It was like She could see me, and I could see Her. I felt Her love, Her warmth, Her power, Her majesty, Her beauty—everywhere I looked, She was there. Everywhere I turned.

My husband and I climbed "The Path of the Gods", about 2000 feet above sea level. At one point in our descent, I needed to climb down a steep staircase. On one side was the side of the mountain, and the other was a straight drop down to the sea below. It was windy. I felt afraid. I felt a sensation of birth, just before a baby emerges into the world during delivery: "Can't go forward. Can't go back, either." The Spirit gently whispered instructions to guide me safely down, and I felt it was the Spirit speaking for Her.

I know that She will always be here to carefully direct me in this earthly sojourn, whether it's 2,000 feet above the Mediterranean Sea or at home doing scripture study with my family.

On this trip, I saw Her beautiful face in each woman that I met (women from all over the world!) and in the beauty of the land. I felt Her. She is a force of love beyond anything I have experienced before. Now I feel Her all the time. I know that She is real and that She loves each of us so tenderly and so powerfully.

Ashli Carnicelli

Family Councils

President Ballard has taught much about the importance of family councils. Generally, such significant earthly rituals are patterned after heavenly ones. Therefore, while I always direct my prayers to Heavenly Father in the name of Christ, if I feel I need a full family council, I ask Him to invite my Mother and Elder Brother into the conversation. Ideas flow! I can't often tell which idea is from which loving family member, but I love thinking of all of Them gathered together, working for my good.

Lecia Crider

> "I testify that we are sons and daughters of exalted Heavenly Parents. Knowing our identity fortifies us against our culture of comparing, complaining, and criticizing. As we consistently strive for refinement in our dignity and demeanor as disciples of Jesus Christ, our confidence will 'wax strong in the presence of God.' And we will be blessed with an abundance of the Spirit, with personal revelation, and with an increased love of God and our neighbors."

Sister Rebecca L. Craven, counselor in Young Women general presidency, 2018-23[26]

---

[26] Rebecca L. Craven, "The Dignity and Demeanor of Discipleship," BYU devotional, Provo UT, October 19, 2021.

Heavenly Doula

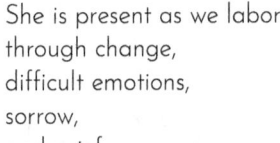

She is present as we labor
through change,
difficult emotions,
sorrow,
and grief.

She is there at the birth
of ourselves
into a new creation.

Angela Ricks

A Circle of Mother's Love

Ashley Thornton

Such An Experience

As a boy of 9, I became lost in the mountains, separated from my family on an overcast night with no flashlight to find my way back to safety. There was not even enough light to see my hand in front of my face. After stumbling about for an extended period of time, trying to find some way out of the darkness, I fell onto a dry stream bed. I was more than desperate as I came to my knees on the rocks. I cried out, "Heavenly Father, I am lost! Please! Please! Please! Help me!" with words that filled the darkness around me but could never reach a human ear.

Only a moment passed and I found that I had been moved to the top of a ridge. I could see the light from the small structure where I knew I would find my parents.

The next morning, I retraced my path from the night before by finding my lost sandal that had come off one of my feet when I fell at the stream bed. When I picked up my sandal and viewed the spot hundreds of yards away where I was moved to, the awareness of the reality of a Father in the heavens pierced my soul. The sense that my Eternal Father was with me that night has never left me since.

I would like to think that I could have such an experience with my Heavenly Mother before my mortal years come to a close.

David Russell

What Chinese Traditional Medicine Taught Me

~

Lord, is this too out there?

You know how your Mother is

Yes

Yes I do

Don't I

We all do

She will heal Her children

However She can

Always

Chelsea Bowen Bretzke

Mother Earth

Kayla Becknuss

The Beauty of Creation

I experience Heavenly Mother in the beauty of creation, in the silence of space that I can feel in my bones when I look through a telescope at Saturn, or in the love that springs into my heart when an old friend calls right when I need it.

Specifically, I sense that She is part of the strength I draw from these experiences when I then have to turn and face hard things. It's like a phone call from Mom because She knows you have that big interview coming up and She wants to make sure you go into it confident in the unshakable foundation of Her love.

Taylor Webb

Her Voice

It's a quiet loud

it rustles the trees

For a moment it seems

silent

then softly

a whisper into my hair as it flies

I love you.

Olivia Bown Flinders

Tree Portrait

How do we increase connection to God our Mother—uncover, discover and connect with Her? This tree portrait uses imperfect circles forming one great whole with the trunk. Most are connected to each other as Venn diagrams (thank you Annie Kershisnik Blake) and where that connection takes place I used a pearl metallic powder mixed with medium to show the extra power of commonality/overlap. Some are not connected but are surrounded. I used a process of subtraction to uncover the white canvas beneath so that the leaves are simple and clear, not because anything was added layered on top of them, but because their truth and beauty were uncovered, exposed and made clean. Most of my work uses bold color for the composition, but this one intentionally lacks it—using gray as a statement in itself.

Julia B. Blake

> "When we sing that doctrinal hymn and anthem of affection, O My Father, we get a sense ... of our Heavenly Mother, and knowing how profoundly our mortal mothers have shaped us here, do we suppose Her influence on us as individuals to be less if we live so as to return there?"

President Spencer W. Kimball[27]

---

[27] Spencer W. Kimball, "The True Way of Life and Salvation," April 1978 general conference.

She's Everywhere

I watched you touch the wheat grass, and smell the forget-me-not.

Everything that was eye level at two.

I felt how fleeting that sweet little slow-down would come to be.

There's a Mother watching me watch you, growing the forget-me-nots.

Showing me everything at eye level in my mothering years.

She knows how fleeting my time away will come to be.

She knows some days feel much longer in my heart.

She sends forget-me-nots.

Maddie Daetwyler

The Woman Whose Presence Lingers

If I had the talent to paint a portrait
of the Woman whose presence lingers in
the quiet moments,
the angry moments,
the awe-struck moments when the lanterns
fail to keep the night at bay,
I'd show you a Woman whose wit and intellect
will make you laugh
in the same instant they make you reflect
on the part of your soul
that is still afraid to dream the dreams
that you once shared with Her.

You'd see the glint in Her eyes;
how it colors Her gentle smile,
suggesting that She sees how the tears you shed
while wrapped in Her arms
are signs of the spirit She knows so well

as it reaches out to fill the space
that it has the strength to fill.

The Divine Feminine I know
is confident and complete.
She would playfully make faces at me
while patiently sitting for the portrait
I have not the talent to paint.

Where Her partner touches my heart,
She touches my weary mind, and
shows me the beauty of the world She made.
She challenges my confident assertions, and
calms my racing mind with the melodies I've lost
since I left Her side.

Nathan Young

In Her Image: Norway

Anita Eralie Schley

Listen To Me Sing

In April 2019, I eagerly downloaded Sara Bareilles' new album, Amidst the Chaos. I was excited to have something new to listen to during my workday.

I was having a perfectly fine, normal day, enjoying the album, when song number eight – Orpheus – started playing. A gentle guitar strummed the opening peacefully before Sara started singing. After the first two lines, I felt a sudden rush of emotion and it was no longer Sara singing to me, but my Spirit whispered that this song was a gift to me from my Heavenly Mother.

I could hear and feel Her voice reaching to me through music and the lyrics. She called me Her "love." She invited me to "come by the fire" and "lay down my head." She encouraged me to not give up trying to find Her "amidst the chaos." She simply offered

Her comfort and Her presence to me, saying, "Come ... listen to me sing."

Until that moment, I had felt glimpses of Heavenly Mother's presence in my life, but on that spring day, She undeniably touched me. Since then, She has used music on a number of occasions to offer connection and remind me that I am Her son and that She loves me.

Chris Sorensen

The Divine Feminine: Her Comfort

Kiley Yates

A Mother

My baby cries and I feel a familiar sensation in my breasts. We are connected in a way that I have the nourishment she needs.

I'm too tired.

My husband picks her up and tries to comfort her. She stops crying but fusses around.

She sees me and smiles, reaching for me. I open my arms and she finds her way to my breast. She closes her eyes and rests.

I look at her face and feel her hand against my skin.

She needs me. Only I can give her what she needs in this moment.

I close my own eyes and rest my head against the chair.

I too need my Mother. Only She can give me what I need sometimes.

Camilla Rodrigues

The Passing Clouds

Jennifer Alvi

Seeking Heavenly Mother

Seeking Heavenly Mother,
I wander slowly along the shore, and gaze toward the horizon.
Heaven calls to me as I listen for Her voice, and seek Her presence here.
I see Her breath in the misty waters washing over me,
I see Her eyes in fractured rays of the sun.
I hear Her voice in both the waves and the silence.
My soul rejoices in shells, love-notes I find at my feet.
She knows just how to reach me, to speak to me.
I listen.
My breath and my heart sync with the rhythm of Hers.
I turn my face heavenward, I soften.
I lift my hands in gratitude and prayer.
She's walking beside me, my spirit is remembering.

Tammy Zufelt Thomas

Finding Balance

Intellectually I had always accepted that I had a Heavenly Mother but now I knew Her spiritually as I had always known Her. She was familiar. The joy of reunification and of being so intimately loved electrified my soul.

I pranced around my empty house listening to music and then ran into my backyard and stood looking at the night sky. I felt She wanted to dance my dance with me and adore and explore the whole spectrum of creation together.

Something else happened which is harder to explain — I began to feel more balanced, as if I'd been living spiritually lopsided, but now things were more even. I prayed to Heavenly Father and thanked Him for this experience and asked if I could continue to draw even closer to my Mother.

Frazer Cluff

10

Connection

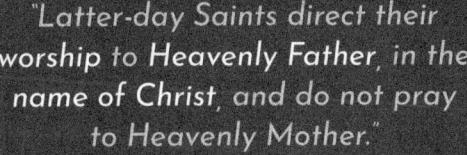

"Latter-day Saints direct their worship to Heavenly Father, in the name of Christ, and do not pray to Heavenly Mother."

~ Mother in Heaven essay, paragraph 5

Substitution

I've sometimes substituted my own name for that of Alma, Mary, or Emma in scripture, but I'd never thought of substituting Heavenly Mother for God, the Lord, or Heavenly Father.

Today, I went to the temple and imagined it as Her house as well as God the Father's and Jesus's house. I imagined the celestial room as being in the presence of God the Father, God the Mother, and Their Son Jesus Christ. It was delicious. Nothing about it felt heretical or out of bounds; I felt like I was on solid doctrinal ground. Of course the temple is Heavenly Mother's House too.

And when I needed a name for Her along with Elohim and Jehovah, why, I used Evelyn, of course.

Marci McPhee

Mother in Heaven and Baklava

For a "Women of the Old Testament" activity in November 2022, I prepared a section on glorious Mother Eve for the program.

The night before the activity, as I was meticulously layering phyllo dough, butter, nuts and spices, I felt I needed to instead present on Heavenly Mother. As the flaky layers baked, and the honey with orange zest simmered, I gathered my thoughts. I found in my margins, notes of Hebrew grammar that made space for Heavenly Mother. Elohim, Spirit, Breath, Wisdom, etc. I printed the Gospel Topics Essay, "Mother in Heaven."

I placed the Eve presentation, my study bible now flagged with sticky notes, and the six paragraph essay in my bag. I cut the baklava, poured the honey syrup, listened to it sizzle and crackle, and went to bed with the sweet smell of honey and spice in the air.

The night of the activity, I started reading:

"The Church of Jesus Christ of Latter-day Saints teaches that all human beings, male and female, are beloved spirit children of heavenly parents, a Heavenly Father and a Heavenly Mother. This understanding is rooted in scriptural and prophetic teachings about the nature of God, our relationship to Deity, and the godly potential of men and women. The doctrine of a Heavenly Mother is a cherished and distinctive belief among Latter-day Saints."

I began to cry when I felt a firm, strong, Motherly arm wrap around me. She came to support me as I attempted to share where I found Her. I felt truth. I felt love. I knew She was real, and there. She smells of honey and spice to me, and when I miss Her, I eat baklava.

Brecken Cook

What Elizabeth Taught Me

∽

Mother
is also
a sister
the kind that is also
a friend

The kind that sits shotgun
Parked in a driveway for hours
Talking
Listening
Laughing
And crying
With you
For you (getting quite worked up if necessary)

She plops down beside you on the couch and says
"here I am!
This is me!"
Revealing Her whole heart
No hesitancy
Like a toddler who figures out the zipper on

her jammies
Or an exploding, glorious star

Either way
She will not be contained
She will not be veiled
Her light always shines through

She grabs your hand
And Her excited eyes say
Now then — your turn!
Who are you?!?

She wants to know
(She already does
Sees you so clearly it makes you gasp)
But She likes to hear
Your version
Your voice
Your telling

You see

Cherish

Mother doesn't just love us.
She likes us.
Close.
Chatty.
Silly even.
Feeling like ... us.

Which is Her greatest gift, after all
When She's with you
You are so — you

Cuz sometimes we miss ourselves
She gets us reacquainted
Says
"Oh you'll like you! She's wonderful."
And we believe Her.

Sitting in a driveway in the moonlight
Watching the fireflies.

Chelsea Bowen Bretzke

A Little Bird Told Me

Fiona Phillips

Bicycling and a Big Dose of Heavenly Mother

"Let me tell you what I think of bicycling. I think it has done more to emancipate women than anything else in the world. It gives women a feeling of freedom and self-reliance. I stand and rejoice every time I see a woman ride by on a wheel ... the picture of free, untrammeled womanhood." Susan B Anthony [28]

Whenever I need to feel an extra big dose of Heavenly Mother's love, I hop on my bike. Almost as soon as I start pedaling, I feel free, I feel powerful, I feel invincible, I feel divine. As my heart throbs and my legs burn and the wind whips my face, I feel Her close by—cheering me on in the wild ride of life.

---

[28] Susan B. Anthony, *The New York World*, February 2, 1896 (Page 42, Column 3).

Hallelujah for Heavenly Mother and bicycles!

Bethany Brady Spalding

When I First Saw My Mother

It was a cold, rainy day in February and in some desperation to escape the confines of the house, I packed my four small children into the car and we drove to visit BYU's Museum of Art. The dull, gray skies seemed a reflection of my existence: tired, lifeless, spent. The spark of the person I was before motherhood was hidden behind clouds of caregiving and self suppression.

Wasn't this the life I wanted? I was doing motherhood as I thought I was supposed to. I was disappearing in my attempts to be a supportive wife and mother. I was hollowed out. Perhaps I subconsciously started to believe that to be a good woman (or at least a good mother) is to disappear. Disappearing women were all around me. I knew every middle initial of the Quorum of the Twelve Apostles but could name only a handful of their wives. As I went to the temple (before recent changes to the endowment presentation), I began to notice all the ways Eve was silent, secondary, and supporting cast.

Walking into the museum, we approached a large painting I had never seen before. It made time stop for an instant. I had to catch my breath and hold back tears. There in front of me, in swirling browns and golds, was Mother—and She was magnificent. She was glorious and good. She wasn't invisible, silent, or secondary.

In that moment, as I stared up at Her, I became aware of the ache that was so deep in me for connection with my Heavenly Mother. I realized I had missed Her feminine wisdom, Her feminine strength, and Her assuring presence in my feeble attempts at motherhood. The painting was J. Kirk Richards' "Breath of Life." It depicts the creation of Adam, but it began the rebirth of me. I began a journey of growth and healing, as I slowly learned to substitute disappearing and dullness with discovery and development. I treasure that day, five years ago, when I first saw my Mother.

Elizabeth Lochhead Crittenden

Tending the Seeds of Life

When we plant a physical seed and hope for it to grow, we make sure it is getting sunlight and regular watering. We will tend the seedling as it sprouts and continue to nurture it until it bears the desired fruit. That fruit or vegetable nourishes and helps us to grow physically and become stronger.

When we plant a spiritual seed, we must similarly give it light, regular "watering," and the attention needed for its development. It takes time for roots to form and create a solid foundation for the flowering plant. This is underground work, done in the dark and in the stillness. A seed never becomes a plant or a tree without one — or many — growing seasons. Don't be in a rush. Plant your spiritual seeds, lovingly tend to them, and patiently await the harvest.

How do we plant the seed of the doctrine of Heavenly Mother?

    read the Gospel Topics essay and ask in prayer to more fully understand the doctrine

    pray and ask Heavenly Father how He feels about Heavenly Mother

    pray and ask for eyes to see Her in the world and people around you

How do we water and tend to the growing plant?

    express gratitude in your prayers for the knowledge of Heavenly Mother when you think of deity, start thinking of Heavenly Parents to include Her

    when you feel the love of God, remind yourself that it includes the love of your Heavenly Mother

As I have planted this seed in my spiritual life and watered and nurtured it, I have seen a bounteous harvest of greater love for myself and others, deep connection to my fellow sisters, expanded knowledge of the power and beauty in the feminine, and a personal relationship with both my Heavenly Parents.

Rebecca Young

Heavenly Mother is With Me

Ashley Mansfield Hoth

Awareness

Heavenly Mother is not the trees when I'm hiking, just as Jesus is not the cross I wear or the bread and water I partake each week, and Heavenly Father is not the prayers at my bedside. But slowing down amongst the trees has become a way for me to sense Her. I feel the life She gives in the oxygen that fills my lungs, bringing life to my body. I feel Her protection in the shade, always present no matter how scorchingly hot the trials of life. I feel Her safe embrace in the strong trunk and branches I lean on or even climb into to rest when I can't move forward. I see Her compassion in the leaves that fall and die to give nourishment and life to the forest. Each is freely given for all without transaction or expectation, whether we are aware of or even acknowledge Her.

It hurts to think that for decades, I was not aware and did not acknowledge Her part in these gifts. But it fills my soul with joy now to see, feel, and receive these gifts more completely, knowing that She was there all along and will be there forever.

Jeff Andersen

I Look For Her

I look for Her

Like a child lost in a supermarket

I look for my Mother

I look around me and hear angry voices

I look behind me and see no trace

I look up and hear Her lullaby

Crooning to soothe Her worried child

"I am here"

"I am here"

Alyssa Wilkinson

Symbol

I saw Mother in the rain this morning.

An image came to my mind as I walked,

face tilted upwards:

My body pulled open to let in the rain,

soothing my nerves and deeper,

cleansing my spirit

and washing away the noise.

Megan Thompson

In Her Image: Samoa

Anita Eralie Schley

Art Show

I was at the Certain Women Heavenly Mother Art Exhibit in 2022. I wanted to be there on opening night to meet the artists. It was a full house, but it was the most spiritually intense two and a half hours I'd spent in a long time. I powerfully felt God with me—God the Mother and God the Father—through the incredible art and written descriptions by the artists. I slowly read what each artist wrote and allowed myself time to take in each beautiful work of art and let God speak to me through each unique medium.

I loved seeing the variety of ways each woman chose to represent Heavenly Mother and to use their gifts of creativity to connect with Heavenly Mother. I especially loved the different ethnicities represented. Each representation was so personal and powerful. I continue to connect with the spirit I felt there as I look through the book of the exhibit compiled later.

I loved talking with many of the artists at the exhibit and hearing more about their creation process, from idea to the experience creating to finished product to hearing how their art affects us. It's a beautiful way to connect with Heavenly Mother—to privately seek inspiration about Her and how to depict that.

I'm so grateful for what this art has done for me personally and how I feel changed and closer to my Mother in Heaven.

I purchased many small prints depicting Heavenly Mother and Father and created a holy hallway in my home with those pictures on one side and Jesus art on the other side. I love how I can come closer to Mother and Father God and Jesus through art as I take the time to let the spirit teach me and fill me with Their love.

Another time, I attended an art exhibit at

Rose Datoc Dall's house. My daughter and I turned a corner and both stopped in our tracks when we saw a large new painting of a woman approaching Heavenly Mother. Neither of us spoke. We were held in a sacred silence.

The emotion was palpable and strong. Tears came to my eyes and my heart was full of awe and love as I experienced what felt like approaching my Mother God. It's something I can't explain, but I express my gratitude for Rose for her gifts of creating an opportunity for me to feel my Mother's presence through a painting.

Jill Freestone

Native Tongue

~

I have found it difficult to change my native tongue to be more inclusive of our Heavenly Mother. As a new missionary in the Philippines, I had to translate what I wanted to say from English to Tagalog. This, at first, was a significant struggle and I could feel the dissonance in my brain.

I am 35 and have been trained to identify divinity as masculine. I feel that same dissonance when I use more inclusive terms in discussions with my friends and other members. What strikes me most is that I don't feel that same dissonance when pondering about or learning about Heavenly Mother. It is replaced with joy, peace, and enlightenment! I yearn to have Her presence more in my life, and the life of my family.

So maybe, my spiritual native tongue is comfortable and recognizes these precious truths, and my cultural native tongue has some catching up to do.

John Adamson

> "Our high responsibility is to become women who follow the Savior, nurture with inspiration, and live truth fearlessly ... ultimately becoming like our Heavenly Parents."

Sister Neill F. Marriott, counselor in Young Women general presidency, 2013-18[29]

---

[29] Neill F. Marriott, "What Shall We Do?", April 2016 general conference.

Mother Nature

Linda Kay Hardman

One Quiet Moment

∾

One quiet moment, in a morning soon full of movement, offers a small connection.

A glimpse of early light, still leaves, and tuning in to a heart that hopes.

I think of the battles of so many I love, waking up to fight another day. Getting babies here, keeping babies healthy, getting through and learning from their pain. Pleading for miracles. They wake up to fight another day.

I know You feel their fight. I know You love them through their fear and their fierce strength. I pray to feel You. For them to feel You.

Just one quiet moment, before the day unfolds.

Maddie Daetwyler

Better Connection

When I think of my relationship with my father, I remember mostly pain and abuse. I have a hard time separating those feelings from my Heavenly Father. Through several painful experiences over several years, I have felt abandoned by Heavenly Father.

By contrast, my mom was a dear friend to me and I had a lot of trust in and admiration for her. I realized I could have a better connection with my Heavenly Mother because of the close relationship I have with my own mom. It made me realize that maybe I could connect with heaven through a loving Heavenly Mother.

John Tullis

Hide and Seek

She opens the door
Peers around the corner
Opens the lid.
The door i closed
Corner i turned
Lid i pulled shut.
I hide
She seeks me
My Mother seeks me
Hour after day
After week after
Month after year
I feel this
As i breathe into
The darkness.

Emily Gardner-Mayberry

Hear Her

Jennifer Alvi

In the Trees: A Series of Poems

~

Seven.

I ran from home, around the block
to the refuge of grandma's house.
I fell into her arms.
She wiped my tears and fed me.
Then I climbed my favorite tree
as she tended to her flowers.
She let me stay for hours,
slumped down in the "Y" branch of that tree.
Resting, regulating, watching clouds and cars go by.
Safe in the refuge of grandma
and my favorite tree.

Thirteen.

Never good enough.
Smart, cool, pretty
enough.

I stepped off the school bus.
My shoes splashed
on wet pavement covered in leaves.
I paused and took them in.
They were massive, still green and vibrant.
Plucked prematurely
from their mother tree by wind and rain.
I picked one up.
It was bigger than my face.
Three times bigger than my hand!
its veins enchanting,
its size mesmerizing,
its beauty spoke to me,
"You are not forgotten.
Your life is beautiful
and so worth living."

Seventeen.

Heartbroken.

Betrayed by a boy who said he loved me.
I walked to the river bank,
sat in my favorite spot
surrounded by trees.
Secluded.
Safe.
I let my tears drop into the water
that fed the trees.
The trees
that in return
fed me.

Twenty-three.

I woke up from surgery crying out,
"Grandmother Willow!"
Repeating over and over how much I missed her.
Sobbing desperately to go back,
back to being a tree that once lived

beside her,
somewhere in my existence.
The Grand-Mother Willow,
wise, guiding, sovereign.
Steady as the beating drum.
Still,
She reminds me
to listen (for her)
with my heart.

Twenty-seven.

I sat in a secluded office
without a window.
On my lunch break,
when the sun was out,
I'd spread a blanket under the biggest tree
and rest.
One afternoon, when the trees were bare,
leaves of all kinds had been gathered together.

A pile taller than me sat beneath my favorite tree.
How could I not?
I jumped in.
Jumped again and again.
Threw giant armfuls of leaves above my head.
Felt them fall all around me.
Then,
smiling,
I pulled leaf after leaf from my hair
the rest of the work day.

Thirty-one.

I moved to a new state,
far from all that was familiar.
The world was in lockdown.
My world was dark.
I found a trail that cut through thick trees

and walked it often.
Each step pulled me further into their world
and away from all the fear that lay outside
their sanctuary.
The path changed with each season,
revealing a new and exciting kind of beauty.
In the fall, the wind swirled the leaves around
breaking them free
to gently float
and toss
and turn their way to the ground.
My feet stopped
and soaked in the magic.
While the company of the leaves
filled the lonely places in my heart.

Thirty-two.

Stripped of all I used to claim "to know"
Questions swirled in my head

refusing to be silenced.
The roots of my identity lay
pruned,
purged,
then set on fire.
Tugged and torn between disconnection,
anger and confusion with my Father.
"Where is She?" I ask.
Then silence,
amplifies the way my heart longs for Her,
my
Mother
God.

Thirty-three.

At my kitchen sink alone,
still flattened by the way my whole world
fell from beneath my feet.
I was washing dishes,

listening to a podcast by women
who seek, who learn, who share their findings
of Her.
I scrubbed and clanked and rinsed,
then heard.
That anciently,
the Divine Feminine
was often represented
symbolically
through
trees.
The words slid into my heart.
I sank to the floor.
Held my face in my wet soapy hands,
and I wept.
I felt Her familiar presence wrapped around
me.
Felt Her majesty,
beauty,
power,

wisdom,
and Her fierce unmatched love,
for me.

She may have been hidden,
erased, or silenced by man.
But now,
now that I've found Her
I see,
She's always been with me,
in the trees.

Amy Nelson

Letter to Heavenly Mother

September 19, 2023

Dearest Mother God,

I've been looking forward to writing you. I have questions. I feel confused, and my soul aches for answers. Since I was little, I've been told by others who I should be. They tell me the things that girls can do but mostly the things we can't. In just three words, they've whittled me down to an insult; "like a girl."

Who am I meant to be, both as a woman and as a daughter of Gods? I go to church and am instructed as to how a righteous woman should act, with specific qualities, desires, and behavior. But Mom, what if I don't fit that mold? Am I still a righteous woman? I have hopes and dreams of serving in your kingdom and doing good through my career. I don't want to give those up. They are good, and I am good. So I am coming to you.

Will you send me your wisdom? Will you help me understand what it means to be female? Please, teach me of my divinity within and how to express it. Help me understand.

I love you, Mother. Thank you for responding to my seeking soul. Thank you for teaching me of eternal truths. I've been amazed as you continue to reassure me that you are there, and you are listening. Today I felt that reassurance as you spoke love to my heart for a child, sick in the arms of his mother. I felt it as I stared up at the sky and prayed to Father, and the trees swayed back in response. Heaven is near. Sweet is tis sound, miraculous is its touch, and healing is the sound of your voice, my dearest Mother God.

Until next time, Emma

Emma Newby

Key to Conversion

For a long time, I've found connecting with my Heavenly Mother to be key to my conversion. I found that to be particularly true when I began going through the temple at BYU a little over a year ago. Regardless of our gender or background, we can find strength and peace in connecting with Her.

Ben Calvert

Namasté

I found Her
in my yoga practice.
Gently twisting my body,
connecting to the earth
like a tree.
Like Her.

The instructor says,
"Cover yourself in a blanket of love,"
What does that look like?
What does that feel like?
Then with my third eye
I see Her, my Mother
Placing that blanket upon me.

I breathe in love.
I breathe out love in a whisper
Only She can hear.
The divine in me
Bows to the Divine in You.

Namasté.

Sadie Hanna

Goddess

Maureen Merrell

> "When we sing the song "I Am a Child of God," the lyrics penetrate our hearts. Pondering this truth—that we are children of Heavenly Parents—fills us with a sense of origin, purpose, and destiny."
>
> **Elder Dieter F. Uchtdorf**[30]

---

[30] Dieter F. Uchtdorf, "Living the Gospel," October 2014 general conference.

Found

I was born motherless,
Alone like a feminine fragment cut off
Distant from the divine.

Or so I thought ...

Riding my bike I heard Her in the clapping tree leaves,
the rush of wind sweeping my girlish bangs,
the thrill of speed racing down hills.

I felt Her in the pillar of strength at my core,
the inner compass that never wavered,
the discernment of light.

She pointed the way ...

I danced with Her as my body bore Their fruit,
my arms held tiny bodies linking my heart and soul to my Mother in Heaven forever.

My babies, Their creations, Our great work.

Mandi Lee Taylor

The Navel Mark

My own body is a testament: I have a mother.

She is engraven upon the soft of my belly

A reminder of the constant nourishment she provided.

I think of my first Mother and know: the nourishment never ceased

But flows endlessly.

Carly Roberts

The Mother Embraces the Rainbow

J. Kirk Richards

La Luna

I sat and stared at the moon, one night
(I could not sleep, nor could she)
shining bright, and full,
her beauty largely unnoticed by the world,
but glowing on anyway,
in the dark of the night
her light sparkled on the water,
taking up more and more space
gradually, almost imperceptibly
her shimmering arms extending
to reach me, inviting me into the light.
I sat and stared at the moon
and thought of Mother:
Her light, too, glows in darkness
largely unnoticed by Her children
but She is there—
night after night,
month after month,
She is there.

Danielle Kemp Nelson

Personally Taught By God

The Gospel Topics Essay shares that Joseph Smith personally taught certain women of their Mother in Heaven.

How has the spirit of revelation personally taught you about our Divine Mother? What have you learned? How has that teaching met your needs?

In 2015, Elder Russell M. Nelson's talk, A Plea to My Sisters, awakened a latent need in my heart and encouraged my growth, and further talks reinforced it. Here are some of his teachings that encouraged my personal learning:

"We need your strength, your conversion, your conviction, your ability to lead, your wisdom, and your voices."

"I entreat you to study prayerfully all the truths you can find about priesthood power."

"The Holy Ghost will be your personal tutor as you seek to understand what the Lord would have you know and do."

"Your personal spiritual endeavor will bring you joy as you gain, understand, and use the power with which you have been endowed."

"As your understanding increases and as you exercise faith in the Lord and His priesthood power, your ability to draw upon this spiritual treasure that the Lord has made available will increase."

"He is inviting us to change our mind, our knowledge, our spirit — even the way we breathe."[31]

---

[31] The quotes are from the following general conference talks by President Nelson: "A Plea To My Sisters," October 2015; "Spiritual Treasures," October 2019; "We Can Do Better and Be Better," April 2019.

President Nelson's words invited me into the experience of being personally and uniquely taught by God according to my needs and journey. As I studied, pondered, and acted on these invitations, the Spirit taught me that building a relationship with my Heavenly Mother is essential to my spiritual development.

Jenn Michaux

She Sees Me

~

Once I was having a bad day. The sky was overcast. While I was outside, the clouds broke and the sun shone through. The sun rays filtered through the sky. Suddenly, a realization came over me. I felt seen. By Her. I couldn't help but smile. She sees everyone. She sees me. And She wants to make my day better.

Ashley, age 11

Protection

Renée Marie Foutz

Nature

I connect with Mother in Heaven in nature by seeing the beauty of the earth She helped create. I see feminine power and strength in lightning storms and gushing rivers.

Through Mother Earth, She teaches me to take up as much space as I need, to pay attention to unique details, to make a lot of loud noise or to let things get torn up, broken down, or burned to the ground and let them experience a rebirth.

She reminds me of the value of taking time to create beautiful things. I think of Her attention to detail in all the intricate flowers and broad spectrum of colors and am inspired to spend time in awe and wonder.

I feel the cleansing power of a trickling river or a gushing waterfall, reminding me that Her love is never ending and always flowing, cleansing away the difficulties, rinsing and refreshing me. Water has incredible power and beauty, reminding me to be flexible and flow with challenges, but hold strong to what is true.

I see Heavenly Mother in trees and often I've received inspiration to be grounded deep into the earth like a strong tree. I'm prompted to take the time to let my roots expand and hold me during the wind and storms. I'm told to reach for the sun and grow my branches wide to create a safe shady place for rest.

Watching the moon's changing cycles, I think of Mother God and the times She feels bright and clear and other times I can't see or understand well. I'm reminded by the moon of the divinity of feminine monthly cycles. I learn of death and rebirth and letting myself accept and grow in cycles again and again.

Jill Freestone

The Kissing Hand

~

Based on the children's book "The Kissing Hand" by Audrey Penn

Mom stains her lips brown and tucks
a kiss into my pocket palm. I clutch

the waxy smudge through drop-off,
carpet naps, playground dodge,

ambush, and tap "you're it."
During sticky spills, scraped skin,

tugged twists, and scabbed itch,
I peek at the kiss safe inside

my chubby starfish fist. Sometime
between jam bites and sandy box,

the smudge saunters off, plays

hide and seek so good I crown

her lost. Panic crawls across
plump cheeks. Tears tumble,

then freeze. In the mirror,
brown lips stare back at me.

There's mom's sloped nose.
Her warm stacked teeth.

Her laugh, like a blanket kiss
cracks through my tiny lips.

Alixa Brobbey

Meeting Heavenly Mother

I met my Heavenly Mother in meditation. Although I had known about Her all my life, She wasn't much more than a line in a song.

"Truth is reason, truth eternal, tells me I've a mother there."

When I studied Hebrew at BYU and learned that Elohim is plural, I wondered if Elohim was mother and father, but never spoke of it.

A few years ago, I tried a recorded meditation from a non-LDS spiritual teacher whose book I read. In the meditation, I was guided into an inner temple with the objective of tuning into the heart and finding what was there. As I visualized entering a room in the temple, a woman met me. I remember exactly what She looked like and felt tremendous love and safety in Her presence. I knew immediately it was my Heavenly Mother. I also sensed She has always been with me, waiting with open arms for me to let Her in.

Since then, I have a keen awareness of Her presence. I invite Her to join me in meditation and in spaces where women are gathered. She is a source of strength to me. This taste of Her love has provided me with a peace I didn't have before and enabled me to be more open hearted.

Rebecca Harris Naylor

Meditation On Our Mother

What questions do you have about Heavenly Mother? What things has your heart wished you could know about Her? Do you wonder if She was with you during a specific trial? Or if She watches over your children? Do you want to recognize Her hand more in the world? Do you need Her help with a challenge you are facing?

Take a few quiet moments and simply open up a space for your questions to arise. You might want to jot down in a notebook the questions that come to you.

Find a comfortable position lying down, seated on a chair, or sitting on a pillow on the floor. Take a moment to calm your mind and body with three slow breaths. Inhale and exhale. Let yourself become fully present. Simply make space for you and God to be together.

Set a timer for 15-20 minutes.

Remember, there is no right or wrong question. Joseph Smith invited revelation by asking "ever-better questions."[32] We can do the same!

Begin with one of your questions. Allow time for your mind and heart to make space for God to give you insight, promptings, or inspiration.

At the end of your meditation time, write down your experience and any impressions and thoughts that arose.

If nothing specific came to you within your meditation time, do not worry. End with a simple prayer for help and guidance and

---

[32] Henry B. Eyring, "The Faith to Ask and Then to Act," October 2021 general conference.

leave your heart open to the many ways God can speak to you as you go about your day.

Rebecca Young

11

Eternal Prototype

"Indeed, as Elder Rudger Clawson wrote, "We honor woman when we acknowledge Godhood in her eternal Prototype."

~ Mother in Heaven essay, paragraph 5

Look in a Mirror

~

In sacrament meeting, I noticed a willing young woman who stood to conduct a hymn, but she was unsure of the timing and movement. She looked to her mother, who gave that knowing, reassuring nod and started doing the arm motions from the pews so her daughter could follow.

From my vantage point, I witnessed this silent exchange that spoke so loudly to me. We had recently been talking about Elder Dale G. Renlund's April 2022 general conference talk on Heavenly Mother, and I had a clear thought:

This is our relationship with Her! What does She look like? Like us! What is She like? Like us! "But I want to know more," I hear you say. Then look in a mirror.

Everything we know of Heavenly Father, we know about Heavenly Mother. There might be a different nuance to our relationship, yet She is not an unknown, a stranger, or unfamiliar. She is who we look to when we are not sure how to conduct the song of life we stand before. She gives the knowing, reassuring nod, then starts the movements so we can copy Her. What more do we need to know?

Mother, Mum, Mom for you USA folks, is Her name and being our Mother is Her game! So look for Her reassuring nod, Her silently powerful, "You've got this, I've already taught you how."

As we search for greater truths, remind yourself that you already know Her well, you already have many of the answers, and She is and will always be your Heavenly Mother.

Lorraine Pemberton

Honoring Women

"Indeed, as Elder Rudger Clawson wrote, "We honor woman when we acknowledge Godhood in her eternal Prototype."

This teaches us that it is good to acknowledge Mother In Heaven and when we do, we also honor all women. By doing this, we are teaching both men and women how to think of women. When we think of women as daughters of Heavenly Mother with the potential to be like Her, who is our greatest female example, it helps both men and women respect women. Knowing Mother and Father are equals helps us place women equal to men.

Jill Freestone

Limitless Potential

I am on a constant journey to reinvent myself. I have been so many things ... an archeologist aid, a river guide, a window-washer, a businesswoman, an art curator, a backpacker, a daughter, a sister, a coward.

I mourn when I feel time markers that rule me out—I will never be a go-go dancer or the President of the United States. There are so many things I have dreamt of becoming.

However, one thing I hold onto: my Heavenly Mother is my prototype. She is a God. To me, that means I have the opportunity for limitless potential. THAT brings me peace and joy ... and maybe hope for a dancing career in the eternities.

McArthur Krishna

Revelation

Everything changed

When God the Father broke through the veil.

He revealed God the Mother

To Her children

And bared all the forgotten promises of abundance

And liberated His daughters' long-chained will and potential

To become like Her.

Tracie Frost

In Her Image: Ukraine

~

Anita Eralie Schley

Dimpled Hands

I often wonder if my Mother
Views my imperfect mothering
With the same grace
And adoration
And tenderness
With which I view my daughter
Nurturing her baby dolls
Fumbling
But loving fiercely
Trying
Trying
Trying
With little dimpled hands
Caring clumsily
But it is enough
To make my mama heart
Swell with pride

Alyssa Wilkinson

"As to why we are here on earth, I reminded him of the self-evident fact that, as the offspring of God, we inherit the capability of reaching, in full maturity, the status of our Heavenly Parents just as we inherit from our mortal parents the capability to attain to their mortal status.

"I further explained that this mortal probation provides us the opportunity to, while walking by faith, prove ourselves worthy to go on to perfection and exaltation in the likeness of our Heavenly Parents."

Elder Marion G. Romney[33]

---

[33] Marion G. Romney, "The Way of Life," April 1976 general conference.

Women Who

They say we need women

who instill hope / & encourage faith /
who resist distraction / & learn to discern /
who understand truth / & delight in light /
who breathe kindness / & embody compassion /
who desire to bless / & know how to love /
At the heart of it is this:

We need women
who are more like their Mother.

Lauren Madsen

This sculpture is "Connexion" by Ben Hammond and located in the Utah Women's Walk in Ashton Gardens at Thanksgiving Point in Lehi, Utah. Photography by Lauren Madsen.

The Day I Found Out God Was a Woman

∽

I looked into the mirror,
Studied my female features,
And wondered what part of me
Could be divine.
My deep emotional nature and
Love of the delicate and the fine
Felt swallowed by the
The harshness and heat of the world.
I was soft, I spoke in "maybes,"
I apologized too often,
Where was the power in that?
The day I found out God was a woman,
I looked at myself in the mirror,
Felt a thumping in my chest,
Noted the twinkle in my eye,
And I saw Her.

Kimber Poon

Every Human Needs Her

I am a mainstream, temple-going Latter-day Saint husband and father, but I love and miss my Heavenly Mother. I can't say that I thought much about Her for the first 20 years of my life but She was always as real to me as my Heavenly Father, which is to say, They are both a fact in my life. I was content knowing They were both there and I talked to my Father because that is what I had been taught. I was never mad at Heavenly Father, I just missed my Mom.

I distinctly remember where I was when She first spoke to me (that I know of). I really needed some divine feminine comfort in my life... I didn't pray to Her, but I was singing to myself the beautiful verses of O My Father and the first-person voice of Sister Eliza became my own.

And She answered me. It was lovely and

encouraging in a way precisely like you would expect from an all-powerful Mother.

So I'll tell you why every human needs Heavenly Mother: for the same reason they need their earthly mothers. Can any of us imagine doing away with the mortal mothers in our lives? No! There is a reason why parents aren't single in the divine ideal. We've seen how people make do when the ideal isn't available to them, but nobody seriously questions the benefit of a loving mortal father and a loving mortal mother. They fill different roles here and they fill different roles there. We're all struggling to figure out what those roles are and I do not claim to have any idea what they are. But I do know I yearn for a Matriarch and a Patriarch for this earthly family of ours.

Karl Hale

Sapientia Poetry

You are going to take after your Mother

You are going to be a woman of God

How noble a calling, how suited a gift

She will be in your blood and bones

When you look inside yourself to see

Your eye will turn towards a single fingerprint

She says

"In how I made you, you will see Me"

Anna Rose Foster

O My Mother

Growing up singing Eliza R. Snow's beautiful and much-loved hymn "O, My Father," I was intrigued with the idea of a Heavenly Mother. This hymn lays out basic doctrinal principles in terms of Heavenly Parents. The question is asked, "Are parents single? Thought makes reason stare, truth is reason, truth eternal tells me I've a Mother there."

How could the spirit children of Heavenly Father have been created without a Heavenly Mother? To me, this is mainly why Heavenly Mother is real and vital in the creation of the world and all the spirit children of the world. She is necessary.

We wonder about Heavenly Mother's characteristics because we have not heard any description of Heavenly Mother in the scriptures or modern day revelation. We have a description of Heavenly Father from His appearance to Joseph Smith. But Heavenly Mother remains a mystery and is part of our thoughts and feelings. How do we personally think of Heavenly Mother? To me, Heavenly Mother reflects a loving, gentle stillness. If Her voice was heard, it would be a quiet whisper surrounding us. "You are loved, my child, you are blessed." The way Heavenly Mother must speak to her spirit children.

Heavenly Mother should have long arms as She encompasses millions of spirit children that have been created. Was this nurturing behavior learned by Heavenly Mother in pre-mortal life to help fulfill her role as Heavenly Mother? I believe Heavenly Mother showed us by example during our time in the Spirit World how to be a Mother, how to love. Unconditionally.

Janice McArthur

Mother of All

Jennifer Alvi

Strengthening Women

I seek to learn about strong faithful women in the scriptures, I seek to learn about Heavenly Mother in order to strengthen women in my home, family, Church, and work. The Doctrine of Heavenly Mother resonates with me because I want to uplift the mother of my children, the daughter-mothers of my grandchildren, my mother, my sister-mothers, and church-mothers, etc.

Brent A. Fisher

In Her Image

Ovaries swollen with shots and with shame,
She watches me
wince, poke, and sigh in Her image.

My sorrow multiplies.

Mother, please witness
Your cursed daughter crying.
Mother, just once,
let my body be good.

Sarah Emmett

A Mother's Voice

∼

Oh Mother
how I struggle
to find Your voice,
to know Your face
to hear Your whispers.
Maybe because
the voice of a mother
has always sounds harsh,
always so punitive,
always so hurtful.
Oh Mother,
teach me how to mother,
with no expectations,
unconditional love,
clear directions.
Please Mother,
show me how
to lead in sweetness,
correct with softness,
and to always

allow them to
make mistakes,
by loving myself,
not despite my mistakes,
but because of
where they take me.

Camilla Rodrigues

Acknowledge

Elder Rudger Clawson taught us that we can "acknowledge Godhood in [women's] eternal Prototype." In the absence of more concrete patterns to follow, I reflected on ways we acknowledge important people in our lives and can certainly extend to our Heavenly Mother. Here are some practices:

Make time to listen to Her.

See Her and make it easy for others to see Her in our art, language, and symbols.

Practice recognizing and appreciating Her handiwork.

Spend time seeing specifically what She has done for us, then thank Her for it.

Use the gifts and talents She has given to us.

Accept Her invitations and reciprocate by inviting Her to us.

Not be ashamed of Her. "Confess" is a telling synonym for "acknowledge," which leads me to wonder if I have ever been guilty of treating this cherished doctrine as though it were sinful or heretical.

Emulate Her, when possible. Given that we know precious little, we can prayerfully study the lives of Her valiant children, to discern glimpses of Her.

Exercise faith that we knew Her in a previous world, that She knows us, and that one day we will know more.

Dan Call

The Divine Feminine: Her Love

Kiley Yates

In Their Image

I was always told I was created in God's image; It made me feel so special

but as I got older, I touched my hands—those were not my Father's hands—

I looked at my eyes—those were not my Father's eyes—

I lifted my breasts—that was not my Father's chest—

I placed my hand on my womb—that was not my Father's womb—

my brothers all looked like Him,

but I did not.

How could I be created in the image of God if I looked nothing like Him?

It wasn't until later that I learned

I wasn't created in His image at all,

but Hers.

Danielle Kemp Nelson

I'm Hers

Have you ever had
Someone find out you are related to your earthly mother
They look surprised and delighted

"You're ___'s daughter?!?" they exclaim
You know your Mom is really awesome –
She's your Mom!
"You look just like her!!" they say
or, "Oh wow, no wonder you are so talented/smart/accomplished/kind!"

That's how I feel
Walking through the world
I smile to myself
My heart beaming with pride to be identified and claimed–
"Yes!" I say,
"I'm Hers."

Ashli Carnicelli

Baby Mine

One thought:
"Dry your body like you love yourself."

Closing my eyes,
I see a baby:
Soft skin, helpless,

naked from being bathed.

Mother's touch is gentle,
mindful of each wet toe.
No rushing here,
only moments to cherish.

When the skin of Her sweet babe is dry,
She wraps Her softest blanket around
such tiny features.

Close to Her breast,
I am safe.
And I learn to love my body
from my Mother,
Who looks like me.

Sadie Hanna

> "Like our Heavenly Parents and our Savior, we have a physical body and experience emotions."

Sister Reyna I. Aburto, counselor in Relief Society general presidency, 2017-22[34]

---

[34] Reyna I. Aburto, "Thru Cloud and Sunshine, Lord, Abide With Me!", October 2019 general conference..

First Time Nana

Becoming a grandma has made me ponder anew all the things that I have to learn from Heavenly Mother. I, like Her, am now parenting someone who herself is a parent. My daughter still needs my guidance, my love, and my wisdom but she now has the task of developing her own motherly, womanly intuition for herself and her newborn little girl. I know that Heavenly Mother will be with all of us as we move forward in our mortal journey together and I look forward to the many things She has to teach me as I try to follow Her footprints and channel Her love for my daughter and this new beautiful little one.

Rebecca Young

12

Sacred Knowledge

"As with many other truths of the gospel, our present knowledge about a Mother in Heaven is limited. Nevertheless, we have been given sufficient knowledge to appreciate the sacredness of this doctrine."

~ Mother in Heaven essay, paragraph 6

A Letter To My Bishop

My Relief Society teacher and I decided to cover Elder Renlund's April 2022 talk, "Your Divine Nature and Eternal Destiny" on Mother's Day. Two days before, the Bishop texted asking that we not spend the whole lesson talking about Heavenly Mother, as some sisters may "come away less than uplifted or uncomfortable," and that she also talk about motherhood. As Relief Society President, this was my response:

Bishop, while I understand where you are coming from, here are a few things to ponder:

Heavenly Mother is our doctrine. We know we have a Heavenly Father who loves us, we are taught that from the time we are little. What we aren't taught as much is that we also have a Heavenly Mother, who loves us just as much as our Heavenly Father. What better way to get to know how much our Heavenly Mother loves us than to learn about Her using a general conference talk which discusses Her clearly? If our goal in this life, as sisters, is to become like Her, we NEED to know Her.

Asking anyone to talk about motherhood (because talking about Heavenly Mother might make some sisters uncomfortable) just shifts negative feelings to a different group of sisters. Many sisters don't enjoy talking about mothers for a multitude of reasons. They aren't one, but want to be. They are one but struggle with finding happiness in it. Their mom has died or they have a strained relationship with her, or maybe it's their kids they have a strained relationship with, or have passed on before them. This topic can be so painful for some sisters, many find reasons to miss church on Mother's Day. Your request to spend time talking about motherhood so that someone else doesn't feel uncomfortable isn't a swap in the positive direction.

For years, many of us sat—or still sit—through lessons regarding current understand of doctrine or church policies that we find uncomfortable due to the lack of inclusiveness to our brothers and sisters (any lesson on priesthood ordination and temple attendance before 1978, or the culture/policy against women praying in sacrament meeting or conference because we "can't invite the Spirit," etc). This doctrine of Heavenly Mother is not exclusive in the slightest. ALL of us are Her children, She is our spirits' Mother.

IF talking about a topic so *completely*

inclusive makes us uncomfortable, maybe it is time to reflect, ponder, and pray about that. It is only through uncomfortable times that we grow, be that our physical bodies, ideas/thoughts, or our spirituality. If we just stay where we are comfortable, we won't reach our goals; especially our goal of reaching the Celestial Kingdom.

I think we will all be able to learn something about ourselves, our potential, and the amazingness of BOTH of our Heavenly Parents from this lesson. I think it will be great.

President Carrie Matheny

Eternal Perspective

As I teach my daughters about their potential and value, it is fairly easy to include the eternal perspective. During my sincere seeking to navigate the undeniable good and truth I have found in the restored gospel, I have felt a longing for my Heavenly Mother. I have explored my relationship with Her through study, art, writing and pondering which has led to wonderful experiences and comfort that continues to sustain me.

Taylor Norton

Heavenly Grandmother

Lovely McArthur

The Moon Is A Mother

The moon is a mother, a mother like me,

The way that she pushes and pulls at the sea.

The sweat and the tears are all salt and water

Much like the ocean; and I—the sun's daughter

Will shape life in my belly and also by words,

Through the most powerful prayers ever heard.

A righteous desire, a dream most divine,

The world is a child, and that child is mine.

Jessica Vergara

The Call

I woke up that morning with a start, the picture lingering in my mind. I had been standing in front of a large group of women, teaching. My whole body animated, my face reflecting joy. My husband was close by, supporting me.

What had I been teaching? I remembered the sadness I had felt weeks before in Relief Society as women had declared that God had not granted them any creative gifts. I recognized I had been reminding women of things we had not realized we had forgotten. We have creative power flowing within us. Our gifts and soul desires are unique touchpoints for this divine power.

I wanted to jump out of bed and shout it to the world. But it wasn't time yet. Like Mary, I filed this knowing in my heart.

***

My journey led me to the doctrine of Heavenly Mother, which I had held tightly to from a young age but had not yet explored. I began seeking a relationship with Her. Wise voices nurtured my seeking.

****

Awake during the night, reflective and calm, I pondered the witness of the women teaching me of my Divine Mother. My prior vision of teaching women returned, and my inner voice spoke. I wanted to teach women about the doctrine of our Divine Mother, including how to cherish Her by cherishing ourselves and one another. God's love flowed through my desire, filling me with light and excitement. I knew this was part of my life's work, and I was ready enough.

I love gathering with women and men to speak of Her and offer my witness that She lives and is an integral part of our lives.

Jenn Michaux

See the Divine

Does it make a difference to you to know you have both a Heavenly Mother and Father? Is it fundamental in every decision you make?

Understanding that I am a daughter of Heavenly Parents and that my eternal destiny is to become like Them shapes how I choose to spend my time, how I take care of my body, how I speak about my body, what I choose to study and learn, and so much more. If I am to become like my Mother in Heaven, I have a lot to learn. It makes me more eager to understand a diversity of topics!

Understanding more about Her helps me to more easily see the divine in myself and not see myself as less than men.

Jill Freestone

Embraced

This piece came to me during a guided meditation—we were asked to picture our younger self, current self, and future/perfect self. Each of these parts of myself expressed love, forgiveness, and acceptance to each other while embracing.

I also pictured Mother embracing us, unconditional love and adoration surrounding and filling us. This was powerful to me of pure love and connection with all parts of me and with the Mother of us all.

Amanda Levy

Strong Witness

I consider myself fully committed and devoted to the restored gospel and church of Jesus Christ. I have been yearning to know my Mother in Heaven for years now.

With what I understand from the plan of salvation and modern revelation, I have a strong witness that we have Heavenly Parents—not some single Dad in Heaven.

I don't think I've had a specific experience when I've felt Her or had Her communicate with me, but I have such a strong desire to feel connected to Her in addition to the solid connection I feel to the Father and especially to my Savior.

Brother Heaps

Rumors and Longing

When I first heard that church historians traced the rumor that Heavenly Mother was too sacred to talk about to a seminary teacher from the 1950s, I felt cheated. Fifty-five years of my life following a doctrine that wasn't a doctrine, keeping myself from the Divine Mother. I could have had a relationship with Her and been feeling Her comforting presence. Did that rumor hurt Her too, by having one side of the relationship with Her children cut off? I longed for what I had missed.

Making up for lost time, I endeavor to fill up my longing. I fill it by searching others' words about Her. I look for Her in nature as I harvest my garden, and as I watch the colors of sunsets and changing leaves. I find Her in my children, my mother, my sisters. We are like Her. The joy and intellect and childish delight of searching is pushing out the angry feeling of loss I experienced with the rumor.

There's no room for anger for She is joy, She is creation, She is love.

Lisa M. Foster

> "They that seek, by faith and earnest prayer, find the light that leads to the golden gate. They that knock with study and faith's assurance have the narrow way opened to them and are received into communion with the Infinite Father and Mother."

Sarah Granger Kimball, founder of the Relief Society in Nauvoo, Illinois, 1842[35]

---

[35] Sarah Granger Kimball, At the Pulpit: 185 Years of Discourses by Latter-day Saint Women, (Salt Lake City: The Church Historian's Press, 2017), edited by Kate Holbrook and Jennifer Reeder, chapter 22.

A Gentle Rising Up of My Soul

∾

Leaving the temple, it was dark. The parking lot was lit and my faded chacos splashed puddles as I scurried to my car. Driving through the city streets, my windshield was specked with water drops. The cars rhythmically passed along to my left. I heard women's voices speaking in the background, an introduction of a woman who wrote books about women in the Bible, and conversation about a new book. The traffic and hum of the city faded into the background as the podcast voices came forward; my heart started to listen.

They were speaking about my Mother in Heaven, and about other women who felt compelled to tell their stories about Her. As I listened, it was like my soul began to gently rise up, in that car, on my way home, amidst the congestion and chaos of the world. A wave of small experiences that I've carried around my whole life, moments I have never really given voice to, floated to the surface of my consciousness. And this thought wrote its words in my mind as I listened to the podcast and felt my soul continue to rise:

"Tell her your story, tell her about your blessing."

And so I did. I am so grateful to have a place to share and to learn and to grow. I cherish the doctrine of Heavenly Mother.

Mandi Lee Taylor

Her Arms

My arms around the tree
And when I look up
I see so many branches

Reaching out
Like Mother's arms
So many arms.

Her arms reach out for me
They reach out for you.

They reach out to all.

To the weary
To the heartbroken
To the joyous
To the lonely
To the strong
To the weak
To the female

To the male
To the anxious
To the calm
To the young
To the old
To the everything in between

Her arms continually reach out.
Powerful.
Strong.
Loving.
Oh, so loving.

Lauren Robinson

The Mother Tree: Keeper of Wisdom

~

Jane Roberts DeGroff

Wisdom's Sister

~

In the twilight of the evening
On a dark and starry night

Walked a woman with a candle
Spreading dancing trails of light

Her hand stretched out to succor
All those touched by cancer's call

When the words that shatter senses
Make kinswomen of us all

Wisdom's sister, take my hand
Give me grace to understand

Wisdom's sister,
Walk beside me when I falter
On a path I never planned.

With the dawn the light spreads outward
Granting warmth and life to earth

Lifting hearts and hands together
Giving space for a rebirth

Share the walk and share the wisdom
Of a road both long and real

A simple gift, a sweet renewal
Comes with trusting we can heal

Wisdom's sister, take my hand
Give me grace to understand

Wisdom's sister,
Walk beside me when I falter
And whisper that I can

"Say unto wisdom, Thou art my sister; and call understanding my kinswoman." Proverbs 7:4

Bethanie Newby

Mother, We Seek To Know You

∼

Mother Nature, Your archetype. If You are akin to Mother Earth and land that sprouts, You must be found in the water as well. Water is communal and bonding; all sources of life gather around, partaking for sustainment. Communities form, resources shared, gatherings expand, nurturing rendered. Your boundless love binds every race, orientation, and lung that breathes.

Water is mutable and expansive, converting to power. Water is patient and tenacious, until it has carved its way through breath-taking passages. And most importantly, water is mandatory for the sustenance of life. Your Spirit is mighty enough to power the world and small enough to dribble into a thirsty mouth.

Water is symbolic of emotion; energy that flows until it reaches an outlet. Water fills space to its full capacity. When the clouds are too heavy, water drips to the Earth. Water is the output of a tearful cry, of a soul wrenching in pain. You are a boundless container of emotional expression, holding the world's cries all at once in Your embrace. You are grand enough for the entire capacity of human expression.

Water is nurturing. In moments of despair, short breath, or light-headedness, water is provided. A healing balm of refreshment to gulp down, comforting and soothing the body. Water is abundant with resources found in its flow. As life needs water to stay alive; our souls need Your power, expression, and nurturing.

To our daily need of water; we have daily need of You.

We seek to know you, Mother.

Chantel M. Day

Midnight Prayer

"Heavenly Father,
Do you love me?"

"Of course I do."
Comfort. Clarity.

"Heavenly Father,
Do You love Heavenly Mother?"

I felt Father's joy as He responded,
"Yes. More than you can comprehend.
She is my delight.
I love Her with an eternal, perfect love."

Malinda Wagstaff Metro

More Words

I cannot wait to have more words to accurately describe our Heavenly Mother.

We can name many different roles and titles for the Divine Masculine, embodied by both Christ and God the Father—Creator, Friend, Almighty, Councilor, Prince of Peace, and, of course, Father.

The only word we have for the Divine Feminine is Mother. I pray for the day when we have divine reinforcement for what we've known all along—that women are more than just mothers and future mothers.

Nathan Young

In Her Image: Vietnam

Anita Eralie Schley

Three Simple Lines

～

I'm here.

I hear you.

I love you.

Three simple lines

played over and over again in my mind —

Her voice is so beautiful,

familiar,

resonating

I know You're here, Mother.

I hear You.

I love You, too.

Channing Olivia Hyde

Two Mothers – Side By Side

Two Heavenly Mothers,
one on my left, one on my right.
Their presence radiates in and through me,
breathing life into my seeking.

Heavenly Mother,
who surrendered me to life.
In the releasing,
She gave me Her heart with grace.

Earthly mother,
the one of my birth,
held my hand, and taught me to pray.
She anchored my faith.

Here in the still shadows of night,
I look up to the sky.
There is an ache,
sometimes so deep it takes my breath away.
The remembering of them

keeps me seeking,
helps me to move forward,
with hope and faith.

The heavens pour out their light through the stars.
I think of Their eyes,
how They watch over me,
when my hope feels shattered by the night.

My soul remembers, how They held me close,
not wanting to let go,
but knowing
it was a journey I needed to take.

My heart remembers They loved,
how They still do.
The remembering sustains,
and gives strength to go on.
Now in the solitude of dawn,

the sky painted a brilliant red-orange,
I embrace my journey, renewed,
as we walk side by side.

Tammy Zufelt Thomas

Praying for Wisdom

As a child I prayed for wisdom
Later I learned that She is Wisdom
And I understood what I had wished for so fervently—
was Her.

Angela Ricks

> "Within every human body dwells a living spirit born to our loving, eternal Heavenly Parents. When parents know this, they can better guide their families by focusing upon the eternal relationships and the true purposes of this life."

Elder M. Russell Ballard[36]

---

[36] M. Russell Ballard, "Spiritual Development," October 1978 general conference.

Different Backgrounds

~

"Do you know about Heavenly Mother?" A young woman from Mainland China had stopped me on campus at the university I attend in Hong Kong, requesting my participation in her survey. Her singular question both excited and surprised me, and I paused for a moment to contemplate how to respond. I wanted my reaction to reflect what I teach my son: that we are children of Heavenly Parents, that having a Heavenly Mother is as real and normal as having a Heavenly Father.

"Of course!" I replied, as nonchalantly as I could, eliciting a response from her that mirrored my own surprise. She asked how I knew about Heavenly Mother. I spoke to the teachings of Christ's church, and to the reality that if we have a Heavenly Father, surely we must also have a Heavenly Mother. I told her about how I felt Heavenly Mother's presence when I first gave birth to my son. She supported me in the first few days of motherhood in a way that mirrored how my mom would support me when she arrived a week after my son's birth.

As we spoke, it struck me how two women from vastly different cultural and religious backgrounds had come to know of Her reality. This young woman, like me, must have also felt Her guidance and love. Like Heavenly Father, our Mother is no respecter of persons and Her presence is universal to all.

Ashley Stevens Chenn

Eve Yearned To Be Like Her Mother

~

Renée Marie Foutz

What Denita Taught Me

Here's what I think

And why I don't have a problem with it

Father is like: "She's the real deal"

He can't wait for everyone to know Her

Cuz She's amazing

Chelsea Bowen Bretzke

New Perspectives

I am in the middle of transforming my faith and am trying to be more intentional with my worship. I have lived my whole life feeling that the "heavenly hush" was God inspired and that not discussing Heavenly Mother was somehow heroic for defending Her. I extended these thoughts of heroism to my interactions with the women around me by incorrectly assuming that not discussing the divine feminine was weirdly protecting the women around me.

I am immensely grateful for these discussions about Heavenly Mother because it has introduced me to new perspectives I was not hearing because of my rigid framework and the culture surrounding me. I have come to see more and more how representation is so important and that examples of divinity can really shape someone's self-worth.

John Adamson

13

Highest Aspiration

"As Elder Dallin H. Oaks of the Quorum of the Twelve Apostles has said, 'Our theology begins with heavenly parents. Our highest aspiration is to be like them'."

~ Mother in Heaven essay, paragraph 6

In Your Image

I exist in the space between

not yet and

maybe never.

You exist in the spaces between

priestess powers of creation

and divine destiny.

You are the essence of fertility,

Eternal Mother —

the giver of endless life.

How can I be You in embryo,

when embryos seem impossible

for this body to hold?

I am not a mother,

but my divine destiny still contains

Your image in embryo.

Your creative talent nurtured

in me, giving life to words

and works of value.

You – true giver of life

& Me – a life given

to the collection of words.

And whether or not motherhood

ever defines me,

it defines You.

And it, like You,

might go unknown in this life,

but remain no less real

.

In my study of Heavenly Mother, I have been drawn to many pieces of art and poetry created to honor Her. So many of these depictions emphasize Her responsibility as Mother. At the writing of this poem my husband and I have grappled with infertility for over three years, and I have found both comfort and pain in exploring my understanding of the Feminine Divine. I wanted this poem to reflect the tension between feeling distanced from Her because of my inability to relate to Her attributes as a mother, while also connecting with the attributes often accredited to motherhood that I do possess—creator, seeker of truth, nurturer. Above all, so much of what we know of Heavenly Mother is rooted in hope, and that is the space that my infertility journey has also had to grow in. Uncertainty tied down by strands of undeniable truth: promised blessings with unknown delivery dates.

Erika Larsen

Stitches

Her fingers guide the needle

Pushing and Pulling threads

Making them strong

And making them feeble

Up and down they go

Up and down I go

She sews back together

The parts that came undone

Through highs and lows

She's helping me become

Camilla Rodrigues

Comfort From Her

My name is Andrew Alger and I am currently a missionary. My family has been exploring and learning about this subject for years, most especially my mother and oldest sister. I want to know more about Heavenly Mother but I guess first I need to have a greater desire.

I know that She is there. There have been times when I didn't have a mother to go to for problems in my life and I now recognize the comfort I prayed for was not just from my Father and Savior but prominently from Her. I know that She wishes to help all of us more , we just need to seek for that connection. I wish to be able to teach my future family about Heavenly Mother so they can help me to explore and discover more.

Andrew Alger

Mother Affirmations

Megan Zabriskie Watson

Ripples of Her Light

Her glow dances into our being,
coming in soft,
even before the invitation is spoken.
We greet Her in the
shadowy silhouettes of the trees,
in the roots and branches,
and in flowing rivers.
The wind trembles with Her presence,
Her holiness illuminates
the shadowy places.
What we seek is what we
behold.
We only have to look,
with eyes, and hearts,
open to give and receive.

We make space for Her to come,

with the fulness,

and depth of Her

sacred and holy divinity.

Our voices, our songs,

our service and love,

are the wings She soars

into a life upon.

Through our own giving

of goodness,

we bring Her into

another daughter's

life.

WE become the ripples of Her light.

Tammy Zufelt Thomas

Asherah

Asherah was associated with sacred trees and biblical wisdom literature. Wisdom, a female, appears as the wife of God and represents life. I wrote this poem for my wife, Amanda.

Absolute goodness
Desire to connect
To ponder and reflect
All you share

Light and truth
To learn and then grow
To reap and then sow
Your wisdom and care

A positive cycle
Full of energy divine
From yours to mine
Awe with no bounds

Imperfect emulation
You are my key
And my soul's journey
Through eternal rounds

Chris Sorensen

She Tends to Her Garden

Kenna Berkley

Hope

Several years ago, my daughter was attending youth conference. I received a text from her asking about Heavenly Mother, as I had shared with her what I'd learned from reading the historical essay "A Mother There," along with the Gospel Topics essay.

Her text came with a tone of frustration because she was wrestling with some comments she'd heard. People were insisting Heavenly Mother was "just a Mom." My heart sank. The feelings that phrase brought up for me were complex and loaded with history.

I have struggled since my early youth to foster hope in being a girl, woman, and mother. I question many things. In my youth I often refused to attend church, yet eventually converted to Christ, served a mission, and was sealed in the temple. Seeing the frustration in my daughter's text brought up my own. I took a deep breath and reassured her with what I sensed she needed.

I hold onto hope through our theology and promises given in my patriarchal blessing: "you have, in embryo, the attributes like unto your Heavenly Mother and the potential to become as She is, glorified and exalted." I believe this is true about me, and all women. This belief keeps me seeking to share goodness about what it means to be female.

At times I've struggled with hope, and often think of the scripture, "Hope deferred maketh the heart sick" and resign myself to that heart sickness. Then one day I decided to find the scripture, and the full Proverb 13:12 is completed with: "but when the desire cometh, it is a tree of life." This is the legacy I pray I'm passing to my daughter through her name: Hope.

Amy Moon

Spiritual Force

My mother was the primary spiritual force in our home. My father was inactive from my infancy. He was a good man, and I did respect him as a father, but I had to look elsewhere for male models of holiness.

It was my mom that taught me how to worship and how to look to Christ. And so, I want to know more about the nature and development of my venerated mother's eternal destiny.

Chris Slemp

The Power of Women

I recently had the profound and sacred experience of supporting my daughter in her first birth. I rocked with her, breathed alongside her, poured water over her belly in the tub, and provided counterpressure as the contractions intensified. The midwife, the nurse, and I surrounded her in every contraction toward the end and guided her as she brought her baby into this world. It was a stunning reminder of the great power of women. There was a tenderness in the nurturing, the encouragement, and the sharing of the burden. We can do hard things when we are given that kind of support!

There are so many places in the world where I see Heavenly Mother, but the most powerful reminder of who She is comes when I see the strength and goodness of women. The generosity of women's hearts and the sacrificing of time and energy to buoy up one of our sisters helps me to know the love, strength, and divine support of our Mother God.

Rebecca Young

Share Power

J. Kirk Richards

The Stew of a Fulfilled Life

Ingredients:

3 gallons of infinite love
4 Tb salt of the Earth
2 cloves compassion
1 pound relationships
¼ cup finely ground tribulation
13 cup self-doubt
1 cup truth
1 whole bushel peace
3 cups mercy
3 cups forgiveness
Laughter, to taste

Instructions:

Add infinite love to a large cauldron, bring to a boil.

In a separate container, combine truth and

self-doubt to form a slurry ("self-awareness")

Add slurry to cauldron.

Finely dice compassion.

Split relationships into equal chunks.

Add compassion, tribulation, salt of the earth, and relationships to the cauldron.

Combine equal parts mercy and forgiveness and fold into the mixture.

Sprinkle peace evenly across the top.

Add laughter, to taste.

Let simmer until wholeheartedness is achieved (~12 Kolob days)

Makes infinite servings.

Serve in small bowls. Not every serving needs to be the same, just make sure everyone gets what they need.

Note: Dear Jesus,

Your Father and I wanted to share this recipe with You. We thought it would be helpful for the big family potluck. Feel free to adjust as You see fit. We love You!

Love, Heavenly Mom and Dad

Malinda Wagstaff Metro

> "At the end of this process [of life], our Heavenly Parents will have sons and daughters who are their peers, their friends, and their colleagues. We also will be gods. We will be able to love perfectly, like Them. We will be able to choose right freely, like Them. We will prize and cherish and never infringe on the agency of others, like Them. In other words, we will be able to be trusted with the powers of a god because we have acquired the perfect love and self-control and attributes of a god."

Sister Chieko N. Okazaki, counselor in Relief Society general presidency, 1990-97[37]

---

[37] Chieko N. Okazaki, *Sanctuary*, (Salt Lake City: Deseret Book, 1997), 59-60.

Inspiration

Great art rejiggers our brains. When I first saw Ginger Dall Egbert's "The Throne of God," I gasped. I realized I had never seen that scene include a woman of equal standing. To see our doctrine made visual — that Heavenly Father and Heavenly Mother are equals working together for the salvation of Their children — blew my mind. Our "highest aspiration" is to be like Them.

When I read the Gospel Topics essay and see great art, I have renewed determination to show up in the world following our Parents' model. I want to live and work and love to BE like them.

McArthur Krishna

We Are In Their Image

~

Kayla Becknuss

Heavenly Mother Meditation

Women often don't love themselves. During childhood, you learned whether or not to love yourself; whether or not it was safe to attach to another person; whether or not it was safe to allow yourself to be loved by others. You learned what you needed to do to be loved and how you needed to live, what you needed to say, and how you needed to act, to be loved and safely attached to your family. I have found that one of the best ways to heal this wound of loving yourself is to connect to the Divine, to Heavenly Mother.

I have a strong testimony of Heavenly Mother. I feel Her near as I help women to love themselves more fully. I think it is especially important to Her for Her daughters to know of Her love for them. She wants Her daughters to love themselves because they were created in Her image.

I have found this exercise to be powerful for myself and the women that I work with. I hope it is powerful for you as well.

Write answers to the following questions:

What do you think Heavenly Mother would say if She could speak to you about who you are? What would She want to tell you? What would She want you to know and understand?

In what ways are you like Her?

What spiritual gifts have you been given that come from Her?

One of the best ways to rewire your cortical processes and nervous system about loving yourself is to write your own meditation, record it, and then listen to it.

In this meditation, start as if you were Heavenly Mother holding yourself as though you were a little baby. Shower loving compliments on yourself as a baby, tell yourself all the things you wish someone would have said to you.

Next, do this as though you are Heavenly Mother talking to yourself as a little girl. Tell yourself as this child how worthy she is. Tell her what she needs to know about this period of her life.

Next, move on to yourself as a teen. What would Heavenly Mother tell her? What does she need to know about herself right now?

Finally, as you are now. What do you need to hear most right now from your Heavenly Mother?

During these exercises, compliment yourself, your physicality, your emotions, your character, your accomplishments, your soulfulness, your mission. Throw in compliments for aspects of yourself that you struggle with. Shower every dimension of yourself with Her love.

As women, we often have complicated relationships with our own mothers. If so, this is a chance to talk to yourself the way you wish your earthly mother had.

This might be very difficult for you. It's okay. Just do your best. You might need a few tries. Deep emotions tend to surface here. Let them come. Allow yourself to have this process.

When you are done writing, record yourself saying these things out loud. Listen often.

Amanda Louder

Balanced Polarity

I do not believe universes can even be created without the creative tension and stability that divinely balanced polarity provides. I look forward to the day when my wife and I, equal and opposite, break open our own newly hatched universe and fill those roles ourselves.

Karl Hale

In Her Image: Wales

Anita Eralie Schley

> "Being as we knew intelligent personalities dwelling in the presence and under the watchful care and careful training of our Heavenly Parents before we tabernacled in the flesh, there can be no doubt but that the seeds of many lofty and holy aspirations were implanted within our souls."

Susa Young Gates, member of Relief Society general board, 1911-22[38]

---

[38] Susa Young Gates, "In the Realm of Girlhood: Lesson V," *Young Woman's Journal* 17 (January 1906): 41, https://contentdm.lib.byu.edu/digital/collection/YWJ/id/12682.

God the Father, Goddess the Mother: Divine Individuals

Like Her eternal Companion, Mother in Heaven is defined by family roles: mother and spouse and conceivably sister and daughter as well. Thus it stands to reason — of Eliza R. Snow's "truth is reason" variety — that just as Heavenly Father is God, a part of our Mother's identity is individual and independent: Goddess. If a divinely curious spirit child were to ask who She is, there's a sense in which She could similarly respond, "I am that I am."

Perhaps because I'm a man raised in modern American culture, my mental picture of God is Him alone, or at least standing apart and elevated from others, poised on some luminous ledge of Heaven, gazing out into the universe or peering down on Earth. Overlay my LDS upbringing, and I also see Him standing beside His Beloved Son in garden and grove.

In thinking about this now, I realize that in my default images of Heavenly Mother, She's surrounded by throngs of young children or leaning on the arm of Her Husband. But if They are indeed co-eternal and co-equal, what confidence and admiration—not just tenderness and appreciation—must He also feel toward Her?

For the women in my family and community, can I support them in their relationships as well as sateguard their sacred (literally, "set apart") identity as beings called also to cultivate a self that, after the anticipated sacrificial losses inherent in a consecrated life, will rejoice in being found again?

Kevin Kline

The Music of a Mother

She taught me to love.

She taught me that love is

staying and

watching and

choosing to

hold tiny hands.

Pausing for small embraces

Listening for the melody of each soul

Allowing them to sing their own song while I dance

... in Harmony.

Mandi Lee Taylor

I Am Capable

I am deeply thoughtful and goal-oriented by nature, which is what led me to a depressing reflection on the year 2020 just days before the induction of my second child's birth. I wrote in my journal:

"2020 was a lot.

2020 was hard

I am tired."

With the release of 2020, I was flooded with intense fear of the impending unknown of my unborn child's life. In a matter of days, he would be delivered with known heart defects, a cleft lip and palate and ear abnormalities. Multiple defects along the midline often point to a larger diagnosis.

Would he live? What would happen to my family? Was I capable?

Unfortunately for me, God works within the context of our lives to speak to us. My particular context included the Disney movie Frozen 2 on repeat. That was the...profound ...context in which my first experience with Heavenly Mother was delivered. (Thanks, Mom).

I felt prompted to listen to the song "Show Yourself" and was overcome with the reality of my divine potential and purpose. Heavenly Mother is aware of me and extremely proud of me (along with Heavenly Father). They love me and know that I am capable of so much.

When the lyrics said to "step into your power," my fears of 2021 melted from me. I realized that my ability to mother this child is part of who I am. I am so prepared and ready for whatever will come. And I can love this experience deeply. I had visions of what our family is capable of experiencing this year.

My son was born with extreme birth defects and remained in the hospital for five months. He was diagnosed with CHARGE Syndrome. My family has been changed forever. We are learning sign language together and take frequent hospital trips. And Heavenly Mother was so right—I am capable of so much.

Anna Crabb

CONCLUSION

Our Mother's Love

"You are literally the spirit daughters [and sons] of Heavenly Parents, and nothing can separate you from Their love and the love of your Savior. As you draw closer to Him, even taking the smallest baby steps forward, you will discover the lasting peace that settles into your soul as a faithful disciple of our Savior, Jesus Christ."

~ President Bonnie H. Cordon, Young Women general president, 2018-2023[39]

[39] Bonnie H. Cordon, "Beloved Daughters," October 2019 general conference.

In the Trees

The first time I felt the presence of Heavenly Mother, I was backpacking in the Shenandoah mountains with my ten-year-old son. It was mid-morning and the sun's rays pushed through the chaos of yellow, red, and orange leaves as we hiked along the tree covered ridge, my son leading the way. A cool breeze skimmed my face and sprinkled us with leaves.

I paused to take in the beauty of the trees dancing, and was enveloped by an impression of love that was distinctly divine and somehow undeniably feminine. I felt planted right there on the trail, absorbing this feminine force sweeping through the forest. I closed my eyes and didn't move for fear of disrupting the embrace of Heavenly Mother's arms around me. It was powerful, but not forceful; infinite, but not overwhelming; divine, yet discernable. I had no words or thoughts in that moment. I just. felt. Love. Distinct Divine Feminine love.

I don't believe She loves me more, better, or greater than Heavenly Father. Both love each of Their children infinitely. But this love was greater because it was complete—infinite love from two Divine Beings. I bathed in my Heavenly Mother's love for what seemed hours but must have only been a few moments. Perhaps that's the only way my human heart could process this perfect love.

Since that day, I've gone back into the trees to seek Heavenly Mother's presence. I've always felt close to Heavenly Father in nature, but something about the trees and the colors and the wind that day helped me to see Her, too.

Jeff Andersen

New Joy: A Letter

Dear Mother,

There should be a special word for the joy I feel when my son learns the name of a flower, uses a phrase he's heard in the right context, or takes off his sandals by himself.

Actually, maybe there is: divine.

Do You feel that same joy when You see me growing?

Love, Marnae

Marnae Kelley

Cheering For Me

I am blessed to have a fabulous mother. In fact, my husband always says if I just default to her mothering, we will be in great shape. He's right.

But I am a different person than my mother and my default on many days is not always to act with her patience. Understatement.

What gives me hope is that I know both my earthly mother's love and my Heavenly Mother's love. They are cheering for me every day.

McArthur Krishna

Heavenly Mother

Nichole Marie

Mother With a Capital M

I didn't truly discover Heavenly Mother until I became a mother myself. I sat in the nursery one night, snuggling my new son and singing him lullabies from the Children's Songbook, when I came to the song, "I Often Go Walking." Suddenly, I couldn't see the word "mother" without it being capitalized in my mind. It hit me that there was no possible way that I could have such a loving, involved, incredible Heavenly Father and not have a wonderful Heavenly Mother who gazed at me the same way I looked at my baby boy—like he contained all the magic in the universe. I realized how absolutely integral my Mother has been in shaping who I have become today, even though I didn't know it at the time. A million memories of feeling Her love, usually through nature, came flooding into my mind. Little postcards from my Heavenly Home. In that moment, my whole life changed, and I will never sing this song the same way again. It will forever be about my Mother with a capital M.

Alyssa Wilkinson

> "The gospel of Jesus Christ teaches that we are all begotten spirit sons and daughters of Heavenly Parents who truly love us and that we lived as a family in God's presence before we were born on this earth."

Elder Ulisses Soares[40]

---

[40] Elder Ulisses Soares, "Brothers and Sisters in Christ," October 2023 general conference.

My Heavenly Mother

I feel Her
As She softly whispers
Into my heart
Her voice echoes in my ears
Her heartbeat intertwines with mine
She is my Heavenly Mother
I am Her beloved daughter
She listens
To the pleadings
Of my heart
She provides comfort
In my darkest hour
When I have no one
To turn to
I can turn to Her
She is always there.

Katie C. Mitchell

The Heavenly Family

~

Kayla Becknuss

Great and Important

This doctrine of a Mother in Heaven is especially precious to me; I consider it one of the "many great and important things pertaining to the kingdom of God" that we believe will be revealed in the last days.

Nathan Young

Cherished

A flutter of my lashes on their baby soft cheek
Comfort and peace for them I seek
My hand rests on their chest
My presence still close while they rest

The deepest of love pure and true
I whisper, "I love you,"
over their hearts
Mine for eternity from the start

Praise and thanks and nighttime prayer
You, My Heavenly Mother are there ...

A flutter of You is near when I'm weak
Your comfort, Your peace, Your love, I seek
You and The Father know me best,
Your presence lingering, while I rest

Your deep love for me, pure and true.

Faint whispers of, "I love you,"
My testimony of You grows in my heart.
Eternally Yours from the start.

To You, I confide
As I mother earth side
Your mist is just within reach
To love, to nurture, to teach.

Ever so near,
To You I endear
I love You forever,
My Mother in Heaven.

Megan Rebecca Guyton

> "We are beloved daughters of Heavenly Parents. God loves us, and as a disciple of Jesus Christ, [we] strive to become like Him. And in our striving, we are loved."

Sister Michelle D. Craig, counselor in Young Women general presidency, 2018-23[41]

---

[41] Michelle D. Craig, "The Beautiful Reality of What it Means to be a Daughter of God," BYU Women's Conference, Provo UT, April 1, 2021.

My Heavenly Mother

~

The cool, gentle breeze, My tousling your hair.

The silence of night, My calming your cares.

The bubbling of brooks, My chuckling laugh.

The falling of rain, My giving you bath.

The crashing of surf, My humming to rest.

The soft fallen snow, My dear heart expressed.

The mountains so grand, My strength in defense.

The rainbow so clear, My diverse love blend.

The colours of dawn, My courage so brave.

The swaying of boughs, My comforting wave.

The thunder so strong, My clap in delight.

The stars of black sky, My protective might.

The warmth of the sun, My kiss on your brow.

The sound of the leaves, My whispered sure vow:

That though you forget, My child so dear,

All these remind you that Mother is here.

Kim Siever

Love One Another

~

Love one another like our Heavenly Parents do and that includes our Heavenly Mother. Just a smile can warm someone's day.

Zara Krishna, age 8

My Mother Loves Me

My Mother loves me.
She loves me with a perfect love
This love is not earned, and
I cannot be separated from it—
Unfailing
Complete,
Pure,
Unchanging,
Constant,
Flawless
Everlasting
Love.

My Mother loves me,
And realizing this love for myself
Makes me love you, too.

When my oldest daughter was small
And another sister came
And then another
And then another
Her furrowed brow,

anguished at the thought of no longer being
the center of my attention—
I told her,
"My darling—
Love doesn't divide,
It multiplies"
This is my Mother in Heaven's love
A love so big it must be shared
Fills me to overflowing
Pouring out onto everyone I meet—

You're Her favorite!
And you're Her favorite!
You?
You're Her favorite!
I'm Her favorite too
The light of Her love touches everyone I meet

The Love of God
Is delicious to me.

Ashli Carnicelli

The Youth

I am a male Seminary teacher, and I was driving and thinking about how to help the youth to understand their relationship with their Mother in Heaven, and I strongly felt Her speak to me:

"I love you, and I love those youth. They need to know that I love them."

Brandon Stoker

Owned by a Mother's Heart

"I am owned by a Mother's heart"

Is that what he had said?

When asked how it made him feel to know he had a Heavenly Mother?

I felt dizzy

I sat on the closest rock I could find and stared into the water,

And recited it over and over in my head.

A Mother's heart that would never stop beating,

A Mother's heart with the capacity to hold all my pain and my joy.

A Mother's heart that never asked for explanations or justifications.

I felt swallowed up

Loved and owned by a Mother's heart.

Sarah Waddoups

Filled With Love

I have always appreciated the doctrine of Heavenly Mother and I have not been reticent in discussing that topic in church. I am just a regular member but I have had a fairly unusual life filled with danger and close brushes with death, as I spent 28 years fishing crab in the Bering Sea.

I developed a relationship with my Heavenly Mom through many long hours alone at sea. I truly love Her. I always loved answering questions about Mom because I have a bright faith in Her existence and discussing Her always fills me with love.

Jake Jacobsen

By Our Mother's Hand

I imagine our Mother

Piecing together a quilt with little scraps we give Her

When we come home She tucks us in

Wrapped in the quilt made

By our Mother's hand

Jessica Day Smith

I Want to Know More

As I listened to music, I saw in my mind's eye snow-capped mountains below me. I soared over the tops among the clouds. I did not see any person but I felt a distinct divine presence as if someone was standing above me. I'm not sure why, but I asked if it was my mom. I then felt as if arms were enveloping me and love was poured into me. The sensation was brief but I know I was blessed with the love and presence of my Heavenly Mother.

I believed in Her existence before this, but I hadn't had much desire to seek Her out. Now I want to know this miraculous being who is there right alongside my Father in Heaven. From that experience, I have a greater desire to know my Mother.

I also have considered what it might be like if the roles were reversed and it was our Father that was the mystery and Mother who was readily available. I, for one, want to know more and I hope and pray that more light and knowledge will be granted to us.

Tyler Young

Finding Mother

Hidden from my life

by rumors men created

I approach now, awed

Lisa M. Foster

Going Home

Across skies twinkling, echoing, reverberating,

Mother arranges reunions & neighbors, including everyone.

Joy expands; never, never abated.

Together extending nurturing, love, enthusiasm. Yes 2

Joyous, open-hearted serenity—infinite, eternal.

Trina Caudle

Home

The womb
of my existence, fleshy center,
holy refuge, is a makeshift home
to a wayfarer forged of my body,
dusted with divinity.
This is you.

Inhaling
rays of light,
I confer with them with
the hands of my threadbare heart
through the tangled cord
that tethers us together.
I give them to you.

Exhaling
into the eye of the urgent ache,
a tightening wrings out my Mortality.
The hot soldering of toil and surrender,
of push and pull,
becomes a disappearance.

There is only you.

Invisible,
another cord connects me
to my own divine Mother
and pulses with life.
She who knows my suffering
and all the suffering breathes sacredness into it.
All of it. All of us.
Me and you.

Hallowed cry,
a greeting and a farewell.
Delivered from the great Elsewhere
through my womb into my world,
and borrowed from the stars,
you are here.
And I am home.

Tricia Cope

Only Love

Have you ever felt inadequate, lacking, unworthy, or like you can never become quite who you know God wants you to be?

Do you look at others and feel like you can never measure up?

Do you wonder how you can become like Heavenly Mother?

ONLY LOVE

Recently I spent some time with my four sweet little granddaughters.

Their faces beamed with love and kindness toward each other. This isn't unusual, they share joy and grace, compassion and charity to all that they meet.

Their countenances are radiant.

As I sat back listening, those four light-filled spirits taught me.

In them there was no guile, only love.

There was no judgment, only love.

There was no frustration, no pride, no criticism, no meanness.

ONLY LOVE.

For each other, for their families, and for themselves.

They walk with the confidence of being divine daughters. They know who they are, whose they are, and they see that in others too.

What if we can have those eyes too?

What if the way to become like Heavenly Mother is simple?

What if the answer is,

ONLY LOVE.

Tammy Zufelt Thomas

Welcome Home

Jennifer Alvi

Contributors

~

> "When women and men work together, we accomplish a great deal more than we do working separately." President Jean B. Bingham, Relief Society general president, 2017-22[42]

Jean B. Bingham[42]

Thank you to Jaida Hancock, who followed a spiritual prompting to offer her graphic design skills to create the layout production document for this book.

---

[42] Jean B. Bingham, "United in Accomplishing God's Work," April 2020 general conference.

Thank you to Roger and Anne Pimentel, whose collection of quotes referencing Heavenly Mother and Heavenly Parents provided many resources included here.

Thank you to all of the contributors for sharing your hearts and testimonies of our Mother in Heaven. The river of the love of God flows freely!

Ashli, Trina, and McArthur

Contributors

John Adamson
Andrew Alger
Jennifer Alvi
Jeff Andersen
Ashley
Emily Baker
Benjamin Bardsley
Kayla Becknuss
Eloise Bell
Kenna Berkley
Julia B. Blake
Zachary Brady
Chelsea Bowen Bretzke
Alixa Brobbey
Karin Brown
Dan Call
Ben Calvert
Jacob Calvert
Heidi Carey-Tasso
Ashley Stevens Chenn
DeAnna Christensen
Mark Christiansen
Frazer Cluff
Jenna Conlin
Brecken Cook
Tricia Cope
Anna Crabb
Alyssa Cranston
Lisa Crawford
Lecia Crider
Elizabeth Lochhead Crittenden
Brittany Cromar
Curt
Maddie Daetwyler
Chantel M. Day
Jane Roberts DeGroff
Amelia Dunn
Chelsea Echols
Elise
Sarah Emmett
Kate Rees Evans
Emily Felt
Brent A. Fisher
Olivia Bown Flinders
Anna Rose Foster
Lisa M. Foster
Renée Marie Foutz
Rebecca Frailey
Eliza Freestone
Jill Freestone
Katie Freestone
Tracie Frost
Emily Carruth Fuller
Darci Garcia
Emily Gardner-Mayberry

Contributors

- Michelle Gessell
- Kayla Gisseman
- Nathan T. Glade
- Josie Ann Grover
- Megan Rebecca Guyton
- Karl Hale
- Caitlin Hammond
- Jaida Hancock
- McKinzie Hancock
- Sadie Hanna
- Linda Kay Hardman
- Ammon Hawkes
- Brother Heaps
- Mari Christina Tomkinson Heward
- Elaine Summers Horejs
- Ashley Mansfield Hoth
- Channing Olivia Hyde
- Jake Jacobson
- Rachel Jensen
- Marnae Kelley
- Kevin Kline
- Zara Krishna
- Lily Jeneal Landon
- Erika Larsen
- Guillermo Lemus
- Amanda Levy
- Annie Packard Lewis
- Mikelle Lewis
- Amanda Louder
- Lauren Madsen
- Brittany Manjarrez
- Nichole Marie
- Carrie Matheny
- Janice McArthur
- Kathleen McArthur
- Lovely McArthur
- Hayley McBride
- Hannah Milmont McCort
- Marci McPhee
- Maureen Merrell
- Craig Merrill
- Malinda Wagstaff Metro
- Michael G. Metro
- Jenn Michaux
- Tyler Mills
- Don Mitchell
- Katie C. Mitchell
- Amy Moon
- Rebecca Harris Naylor
- Amy Nelson
- Danielle Kemp Nelson
- Bethanie Newby
- Emma Newby
- Taylor Norton
- Julio Ospina

Clara Packer
Lauren Palmer-Mitchell
Lorraine Pemberton
Kayla Pennington
Marci Petersen
Fiona Phillips
S. Douglas Phillips
Anne Pimentel
Kimber Poon
J. Kirk Richards
Angela Ricks
Carly Roberts
Lauren Robinson
Camilla Rodrigues
Whitney Rose
David Russell
Anita Eralie Schley
Tyler Sharp
Kim Siever
Chris Slemp
Gillian Smith
Jessica Day Smith
April Sorbonne
Chris Sorensen
Sonia Sosa-Rollins
Bethany Brady Spalding
Emily Spencer
Brandon Stoker

Mandi Lee Taylor
Steven R. Theobald
Tammy Zufelt Thomas
Megan Thompson
Ashley Thornton
Josie Tueller
John Tullis
Scott Turner
Jessica Vergara
Sarah Waddoups
Megan Zabriskie Watson
Andrea Weaver
Carlie Webb
Taylor Webb
Elizabeth Bishop Wheatley
Carly White
Ashley Masters Wilkes
Alyssa Wilkinson
Alexandra Williams
Charlotte Wilson
Kiley Yates
Nathan Young
Rebecca Young
Tyler Young

www.ingramcontent.com/pod-product-compliance
Lightning Source LLC
Chambersburg PA
CBHW052129070526
44585CB00017B/1752